By Youth Communication

Teen Journal

MAGAGING TRANSITIONS FOR TEENS
MAKING THE MOST OF CHANGE

Executive Editors
Laura Longhine and Keith Hefner

Principal Writer
Autumn Spanne

Contributing Writers and Workshop Leaders
Rachel Blustain, Laura Longhine, Nora McCarthy, Autumn Spanne

Layout & Design
Efrain Reyes, Jr. and Stephanie Liu

Cover
Adapted from Alex Camlin's cover design for *Managing Transitions*, by William Bridges

Copyright © 2011 by Youth Communication®

All rights reserved under International and Pan-American Copyright Conventions. Unless otherwise noted, no part of this book may be reproduced, stored in a retrieval system, or transmitted in any form or by any means, electronic, mechanical, photocopying, recording, or otherwise, without express written permission of the publisher, except for brief quotations or critical reviews.

For reprint information, please contact Youth Communication.

ISBN 978-1-935552-72-7

First Edition

Printed in the United States of America

Youth Communication®
New York, New York
www.youthcomm.org

Table of Contents

To the Reader 3
Helpful Words 4
Stages of Transition 5

PART I: Learning About Transitions

Session 1: Welcome! Introduction to Transitions 10
Session 2: Building a Safe and Supportive Group 21
Session 3: Introducing the Tools 33
Session 4: Owning the Tools 45
Session 5: Stages of Transition—*Letting Go* 47
Session 6: Stages of Transition—*Chaos* 53
Session 7: Stages of Transition—*New Start* 65

PART II: Transitions in Action

Session 8: Identifying Your Change 73
Session 9: Tools That Will Work for Me 87
Sessions 10-15: Using the Tools 93
Session 16: Celebrating Our Accomplishments 111

APPENDIX

Transitions Tools Cheat Sheet 115
Sample Transition Journals 116
Alternate Lesson for Session 5 149
About Youth Communication 173

To the Reader

This journal will change your life. (But only if you use it.)

Doing the activities in this journal will give you the power to control the transitions in your life, instead of being controlled by them. For example, most youth in foster care have had to move to new homes and live with new families, often multiple times. You have a right to be angry about those changes. But how you manage and express that anger can have a big impact on whether you get what you want out of life.

We do have to warn you, it won't be easy. Real change is always hard. But if you're willing to put in the time and effort, this journal—and the whole Transitions program—can help you learn how to manage changes and transitions in ways that lead you toward your goals.

How do we know that? Many teens in foster care participated in workshops to help develop these activities, and we refined the program each time based on their feedback. You can have confidence that we've created a program that will really work, if you give it your best.

In the first half of the workshop, we'll start getting to know each other, and learn about the Transitions process—how in every change you make, you generally go through several different stages of transition, and how there are "tools" that can help you get through and deal with the change you're facing.

Then, in the second half of the workshop, you'll have a chance to try out those tools, as you work on a change you want to make in your own life. Each week you'll come back to the group and talk about how it went: What worked? What didn't? What was fun? Challenging? Scary? Rewarding? With the help of your peers and the facilitator, you will grow and change. Most importantly, you will be honing skills that you can use in the next transition in your life, and the next, and the next. You will be building the "Transitions process" into the emotional memory of your life.

In the final workshop, you will celebrate the progress you have made. And you will discover several things. First, you will have made real change. Second, you will have developed skills and insights that you can use again and again. Third, you will be very proud of yourself—and of everyone in the group. Finally, you will feel more confident that no matter what life throws at you, you'll have the ability to respond in ways that helps you achieve your goals, instead of setting you back.

Thanks for using this journal. We hope the program is as helpful to you as it was to us.

Sincerely,

The Transitions Teens

Miguel Ayala
Yuhanna Buggs
Samantha Flowers
Armando Goodwin
Pauline Gordon
Erica Harrigan
Gilbert Howard

Lonnie Macloed
Cynthia Orbes
Michael Orr
Hattie Rice
Manny Sanchez
Natasha Santos
Samantha Yang

P.S. We've included several of our workshop journals at the end of this journal (and a couple of them are included with the activities). If you're curious, they will give you an idea of what we were thinking while we took the workshop, and what we worked on.

Helpful Words

Words About Transitions

Change: Change is what's different. One day you have a job, or a girlfriend, the next day you don't. That's a change. Often change is outside of your control, like being forced to switch homes or schools. But you can also choose change, like quitting a bad job. Change is a constant in life. This workshop will help you learn to manage it better.

Transition: How you react and adapt to the change *on the inside*. A change, like losing a girlfriend, can happen in one day, but the transition—grieving for your loss and being single again—can take much longer.

Tools (coping mechanisms): Things we do to manage difficult changes and transitions. For example, one coping mechanism when moving to a new home might be to spend a lot of time in your room until you feel more settled, or to talk out your anxieties with a supportive friend. In transitions, we call positive coping mechanisms "tools."

Words About Making a Good Group

Constructive feedback: Responding to people in a way that is helpful to them. The more we can learn to provide constructive feedback (instead of criticism or advice) the more successful this workshop will be.

Ground rules: The rules we set for how we get along in the group; these should be designed to promote a trusting and supportive atmosphere.

Advice: Telling someone what *you* would do or what you think they *should* do (in the workshop, we try to avoid this).

Support: Helping someone decide what *they* want to do; supporting their actions or emotions without judging.

Reflection: Thinking about what happened, your feelings, the choices you made, the good and bad consequences, and what you'll do differently the next time. Reflection gives you the power to respond differently the next time you confront a problem instead of getting trapped in the same cycle over and over again.

STAGE 1: LETTING GO

You're in Letting Go if you're feeling... teary, defiant, don't-care attitude, like overeating, anxiety, tired, loss, nostalgic, reckless, anger

LETTING GO

With every change, something comes to an end. "The way things were" becomes no longer possible. So the first stage in dealing with a change is letting go of what you're losing. These tools can help you understand what you're losing, say goodbye and imagine what good would come of the change.

TOOLS FOR LETTING GO:

Seeking Information

- **Write in a journal** to figure out what you'll be losing when you change and how you feel about it.

- **Ask people you trust for feedback** on how you can let go.

Social Support

- **Identify who could be helpful to you** and ask them for specific kinds of support. (Also identify people who are not helpful, and establish a safe distance from them.)

- **Write letters** to people you are or have been close to telling them how and why you're changing, even if you don't send the letters.

Rituals and Ceremonies

- **Make up a ceremony** to symbolize closure, such as making a list of the things you're giving up and tearing it up or burying it.

- Read about common rituals in different cultures or religions and adapt them to suit your needs.

Reflection and Experimentation

- **Write** or think about your problem or situation **from the perspective of someone else involved in the change** such as a trusted friend.

- Identify how you might be able to **make up for some of what you're losing.**

- **Imagine new better things you might get** from making this change.

Identify Who Is Helpful:

I knew I should change schools, but I was scared. I decided that two people, my editor and social worker, would be helpful to me in figuring out what to do, but my family would not be...I feel more in control of what is happening because I am choosing who I want to share this transition with me.

—Natasha

STAGE 2: CHAOS

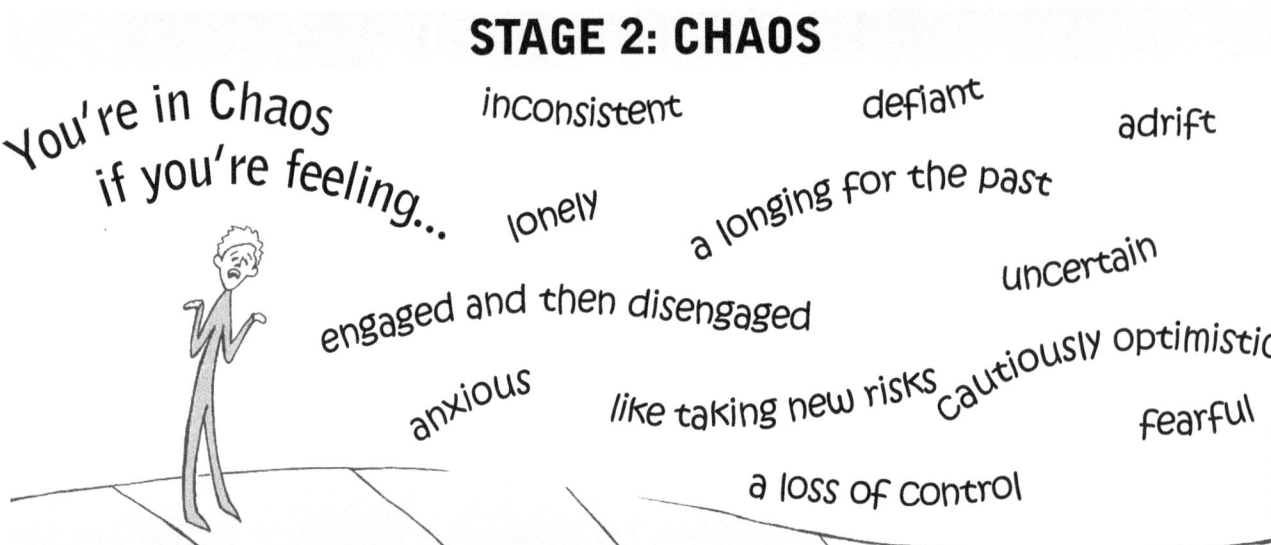

You're in Chaos if you're feeling... inconsistent, defiant, adrift, lonely, a longing for the past, engaged and then disengaged, uncertain, anxious, like taking new risks, cautiously optimistic, fearful, a loss of control

All Art by YC

CHAOS

The Chaos stage is a time of confusion. You've let go of the way things were but you haven't adjusted to the new way yet. The Chaos stage can be scary but also exciting. It's a time when you can explore new possibilities and try new ways of doing things.

TOOLS FOR CHAOS:

Rituals and Ceremonies

- **Set daily or weekly rituals** to order your days during the time of chaos. They could include things like a walk in the park every Saturday or a time you set aside each night for prayer or meditation.

- **Create a ceremony** that will give you a sense of closure on the past, or open the gates to a new way of being.

- **Surround yourself with things that remind** you of good times or make you feel comfortable, peaceful, or at home.

Reflection and Experimentation

- Write notes to yourself asking: **"How do the feelings I have about this change relate to my past? How am I different now from how I was back then?"**

- **Attend therapy** and talk about your anxieties and hopes.

- **Try new ways of behavior** to figure out what might work better for you in the future.

Social Support

- **Search out others** who may be going through a similar change.

- **Ask a trusted friend** or adult for **feedback** on how you're handling your change.

Seeking Information

- **Read a book** related to the issue you're struggling with.

- **Ask yourself, "Now that the old way has ended, what are my options?"**

- **Take a class** or try an activity that might help with your situation.

> **Daily Ritual:**
>
> I read a book called *Path Finder: Real Life and Real Direction*. I decided that one ritual I could do is write progress notes to myself. When I finish reading a passage in the *Path Finder* book I write a progress note in my diary, so when I am feeling down I can look back and smile because I can see how much I have grown over the months.

STAGE 3: NEW START

You're in New Start if you're feeling...

secure
energetic
optimistic
enthusiastic
confident
proud

NEW START

New Start, the last stage, happens when you've really accepted the change and have made it part of your life. It can take a very long time to get to New Start—you might need months or even years to change deep-seated feelings and behaviors. You only get there once you've dealt with the issues and emotions the change brought up. Then the new way of doing things will start to feel familiar.

TOOLS FOR NEW START:

Social Support

- **Celebrate with someone who's important to you.**

- **Tell your friends how you've changed** and ask them to support the new you.

Rituals and Ceremonies

- **Invent a symbol of your change**, like a memento to carry with you, a change of dress, a picture, etc.

- Make up a ceremony to acknowledge that a change has happened.

Rewards

- **Make up** something "official" to recognize your change—like a **certificate to yourself**, or a letter of recognition.

PART I
Learning About Transitions

SESSIONS 1-7

In the first seven sessions, you'll learn about change and transition and reflect on how you've handled changes in your own life in the past. You'll be introduced to the stages of transition and the tools you can use to manage transitions.

Session 1

Welcome! Introductions and Orientation to Transitions

Goals

- You'll get to know the other members of the group.
- You'll understand where the Transitions Framework comes from.
- You'll identify some important changes and transitions from your life.
- You'll get a basic introduction to the Transitions concepts.

Find Someone Who...

You have 10 minutes to ask other people in the group the questions on the bingo squares, with the goal of filling in as many squares as possible. Try to talk to as many people as you can. Introduce yourself to the other person, then ask them a question.

When you find someone who can respond "yes" to a question, *have them sign their name in the square on your bingo sheet* and then move on to the next person. For some questions, you also need to get a piece of info, such as what the person's sign is. Good luck!

Find someone who...

Expects to graduate from high school	Has an artistic talent Talent: _____	Gets excited about change	Has had a job Job: _____	Knows their astrological sign Sign: _____
Has lost a job	Has more than two siblings	Has a pet Kind of Pet: _____	Has broken up with a close friend	Is studying for a GED
Has broken up with a boyfriend or girlfriend	Doesn't like pizza	FREE	Sees the glass half full	Has attended more than five schools
Plans to go to college	Knows what career s/he wants Career goal: _____	Has gone through a big loss	Doesn't like change	Likes to dance
Has made a sacrifice to help someone else	Likes to stand out from the crowd	Is shy	Has a high school diploma	Likes to play video games Favorite: _____

Imagining a Transition: Our Corporate Character

Before we start focusing on a transition in our own personal lives, let's think about one of those corporate executives who this program was originally created to help. Our guy/gal is a top executive at a large company. It's up to you to decide the rest! As we draw our guy/gal on the board, copy down the details of the drawing on this page so that you'll remember this activity later.

Name of "Corporate Character": _____ Age: _____

Name and type of company works for: _____

His/her position there: _____

WORK
(feelings, actions)

HOME
(feelings, actions)

PREDICTIONS
What might the future hold?

CONNECTIONS
to foster care:

Session 1: Welcome! Introductions and Orientation to Transitions

In this story, Natasha, a teen from the first Transitions group at Youth Communication, explains how the process works.

A Method to the Madness
Learning new tools can
make changes easier to handle

Natasha Santos

By Natasha Santos

Last year I made a typical change: switching from one school to another because I wasn't doing well. For me, this change symbolized rejection and failure.

Leaving my school brought up too many old feelings that I wasn't ready to deal with, so I didn't. I spent half my school days in my bedroom, asleep or watching television. When I did go to school I mostly roamed the halls. Some days, I went to class and felt determined to change. But I didn't. It was a lot harder to manage the transition than I'd thought.

Overwhelming Changes

By the time teens are ready to leave care, we've dealt with lots of practical changes, like changing schools and homes several times. So you would think we'd get good at managing transitions, and that when it's time for the big change (aging out) we'd be prepared because we've done it so often. But being forced to change doesn't make us good at it.

Changes bring up difficult emotions and memories that we haven't dealt with, and many times we get overwhelmed or depressed. Luckily, in the Transitions workshop we learned that there are ways to handle changes that we can practice so we can manage transitions more successfully in the future. These *tools* can be helpful and even fun.

New Ways to Handle Change

The first thing we had to understand was the difference between change and transition. Basically, a *change* is an event that happens, like changing schools, losing a loved one, making a friend, etc. Sometimes we choose to make the change, sometimes we don't.

A *transition* is what we go through emotionally, on the inside, to make sense of and adapt to that change. Both positive and negative changes require us to manage emotions.

Using the tools didn't change our past, or the emotions we were going through. But the tools did help us understand what we were feeling and gave us helpful ways to keep moving forward in our lives.

For the workshop, each of us chose a change we *wanted* to make (for example, finding more supportive friends, or being less self-critical). But you can also use the tools to deal with a change that just happens to you, like changing foster homes or schools. Each week we talked about how our changes were going, and wrote a diary about how we handled our transitions.

The Three Stages of Transitions

Next, we learned about the three major stages of a transition:

Letting Go: You first must realize that a change is taking place, and say goodbye to the old way. Recognizing what you will be losing and accepting it is the hardest part, because that often brings up other losses.

Chaos: During this time, you've let go of your old way but haven't yet found a new way, so you have a lot of confusion and fear. It's uncomfortable, but it can also be a time of discovery.

New Start: You begin to feel comfortable and have accepted the change. You're excited by the new goals that you're working toward.

Getting From One Stage to Another

There are coping strategies (we called them "tools") you can use in each of the stages to make your transitions smoother. For example, in the Chaos stage you might use a reflection tool, like writing in a journal, when you are feeling confused. Or to celebrate the progress you've made in reaching New Start, you could reward yourself with little things like a chocolate shake or even a certificate you make for yourself.

Everyone naturally uses some of these tools. When my friend Pauline moved into a new foster home, she used this tool to manage the chaos: "Surround yourself with things that remind you of good times or make you feel comfortable, peaceful, at home."

Pauline wrote: "Living in a stranger's home has been a difficult change. My room is where I recuperate, where

I can gather my thoughts and feel at home. I've framed pictures or have items lying around that remind me of all the people and things that make me happy. My plant I've grown since I was living at my grandmother's house reminds me of warm memories shared back home..."

The point of the workshop, though, was to get us to experiment with tools that don't come naturally, and take a risk to try one out every week to really work on our change.

Trying Out New Methods

For the first part of the workshop we thought about changes from our past that were still affecting us, and then learned new tools for managing our emotional responses to those changes.

Then we picked one change we were struggling with *right now*. We mapped out a 10-week plan of what we wanted to achieve, and the tools we would use each week.

Erica wanted to begin to remember and create good memories. She could only remember bad things from her childhood and often dwelled on those bad feelings. Michael's goal was to figure out which friends he could trust and which he didn't feel comfortable around.

Hattie criticized herself harshly and constantly. She wanted to work on changing the negative script in her head. Pauline worked on preparing herself for independence from foster care despite having little support.

I chose to work on my transition from my old school to my new school, to go from cutting classes to attending them. I wanted to figure out ways to develop relationships with people in the school and also feel more a part of school in general.

Could We Let Go of Old Ways?

We were all excited, but we were worried, too. Could we change? Were we capable of letting go of the old ways that were holding us back? The idea of making a change seems good, but the actual work and that goes into that is scary and uncomfortable. I guess that's why so many people stay stuck in their ways.

We were also uneasy about letting go of our old defenses, and having to re-think some things that life had taught us. Like Hattie: Her parents taught her to look on the dark side of life and to believe that life will always be painful and difficult. By choosing to change and going through the process of transition, Hattie would be saying that the way she had been raised was not OK with her anymore. In a way, she'd be saying goodbye to a belief in her parents and to ideas that had been stuck in her brain since childhood.

Getting Support from the Group

To keep us on track, we met weekly to discuss the tools we used and to give each other feedback on our progress.

Trust in the group didn't come naturally. All of us felt uneasy about exposing so much of ourselves. Michael dealt with this by keeping his distance. While the group sat in a circle, Michael sat about a foot outside it.

But sometimes we really were able to help each other. When Pauline wouldn't admit to wanting to make any changes in her life, we asked tons of questions and then sat and waited until she was ready to open up to us. She eventually did.

And when Hattie was negative about herself, we'd catch her and tell her not to put herself down. After a while, no more negative words came out of her mouth.

Noticeably Changed

Everybody had made progress by the end of the group. Michael began to recognize that his concerns about his friends came from not letting them know what he's comfortable with.

Erica discovered happier childhood memories through conversations with her mother, and took pictures for her scrapbook that reminded her of good times.

Pauline kept herself motivated at handling her job and college plans, and applied for financial support and housing so she could more easily leave care. And Hattie stopped beating herself up.

As for me, I was going to class and enjoying in my new school.

By the end, I think we all felt a little more confident so that when we need to handle huge changes like aging out, starting college, or beginning a new job, we'll have the ability to manage those transitions.

More Ready for Independence

Usually when we think about growing up, we think about practical changes like finishing school and finding housing and a job. But the more difficult changes might be the emotional transitions we need to make inside: From negatives to positives, from bad relationships to stronger ones, and to independence, communication and remembering the good times.

Emotional independence—the ability to deal with our emotions and our problems—is what will give us the ability to handle those practical changes, and it's the one thing no one can give us. We have to learn on our own, by making mistakes, trying new ways of handling feelings we've had for years. Learning the tools, and using them, is a start.

Closing Reflection

At the end of every session, you can use this page to reflect on the activities and discussions. It's a way of remembering the important stuff so you can look back and see how much progress you've made.

▶ What is the most important thing you'll remember about the Transitions Framework from today's activities?

▶ What are some of the changes you are facing in your own life that you might want to work on later in this workshop?

▶ One question you have about transitions after today's session:

Session 2

Building a Safe and Supportive Group

Goals

- The group will start to come together!
- We'll brainstorm ways to make everyone feel included and respected.
- We'll develop guidelines for giving feedback to one another (be kind!).
- We'll come up with a confidentiality policy (what is said here stays here).
- We'll also agree on some other basic guidelines (don't hog the conversation; listen, etc.).

The Counting Game

The goal of this game is for the group to count from 1 to 21.

Sounds simple, right?

We'll play the game four or five times to see if we start to notice any patterns.

Rules of the game

1. Anybody can speak. When the group leader says "go," anyone in the room can say the next number (starting with 1).

2. If two or more people say a number at the same time, the group has to start again from 1.

3. The group cannot use any kind of specific, pre-set order to help them out. For instance, they cannot go around the circle counting in order.

Session 2: Building a Safe and Supportive Group

Giving Constructive Feedback
Advice vs. Support

Adults frequently give teens advice, rather than support, and teens often hate it. Yet, if you listen closely, teens can also fall into the habit of giving advice to their friends, when what a friend really needs is support!

What's the difference between advice and support? When a friend is going through a hard time, it's natural to want to help and give advice. But when you give *advice*, you are telling the other person what to do instead of helping them to see all the options and make the best decision for them. (By jumping in and telling them what you would do, you've made a judgment about the best course of action.)

When you offer someone *support*, you are inviting them to think about their own situation, instead of trying to make decisions for them. That keeps them in charge of their own decisions, which is important in learning how to feel independent and in charge of our own lives instead of feeling helpless and unsure.

The difference between advice and support is in the way that you approach a person. Support means doing things like asking them questions to help them clarify their thoughts and feelings. It can mean showing empathy without judgment—letting them know you can relate and "feel their pain." That feels very different from telling someone what to do.

Look at the chart on the next page. "Advice" is described on the left. "Support" is described on the right. Below those descriptions are examples of the kinds of language we use when giving advice and support. Think about how different it feels to hear advice statements than to receive statements of support.

Advice	Support
Giving advice usually means telling the person what to do, instead of offering them choices. That doesn't help someone think about what's the best choice for him/her. It can also make him/her feel like you doubt their ability to make good decisions. That doesn't help someone feel independent or confident.	Supportive statements let someone know that you are concerned about them, but that you respect their ability to make their own decisions. It can build someone's confidence and trust to let them know you understand where they're coming from without trying to force them to think the same way you do about a problem.
Advice can sound like judging and criticizing: *You should just _____.* *Why don't you just _____.* *You're wrong. Do _____ instead.* *That's not going to help you.* *What you really need to do is _____.*	Support should sound more like suggesting, understanding, respecting: *It sounds like _____ (what I hear you saying is _____).* *I've read _____.* *I've heard _____.* *I feel upset when you say that because _____.* *What you're saying makes sense to me because _____.* *One thing that helped me was _____.*

Session 2: Building a Safe and Supportive Group

Advice or Support: Which Is Which?

Read the follow statements. Indicate which statements are advice and which are support.

"I think you should break up with him."
☐ ADVICE   ☐ SUPPORT

"I also went with a guy who was verbally abusive. It made me feel really bad about myself. Is there anything we can do to help you?"
☐ ADVICE   ☐ SUPPORT

"You should reach out to your father."
☐ ADVICE   ☐ SUPPORT

"What do you think will happen if you reach out to your father? What do you want to have happen? Have you tried to reach out to him in the past?"
☐ ADVICE   ☐ SUPPORT

"When I reached out to my dad it was hard at first, but we made sure to talk with each other each week and we grew closer."
☐ ADVICE   ☐ SUPPORT

"I think I understand your frustration. Whenever I talk with my dad it feels like he's not really listening."
☐ ADVICE   ☐ SUPPORT

"If you would just go to therapy you'd feel a lot better."
☐ ADVICE   ☐ SUPPORT

"I think therapy can be helpful, but it's also really scary to be honest with someone like that. It took me a long time to decide to go."
☐ ADVICE   ☐ SUPPORT

"Of course you're flipping...you keep going off your meds!"
☐ ADVICE   ☐ SUPPORT

"Sometimes my meds make me feel worse that not taking them at all. One thing I've found helpful is speaking up and telling the psychiatrist what's happening so she can adjust the levels and try different drugs."
☐ ADVICE   ☐ SUPPORT

"I think it's stupid to stay in a foster home where they don't treat you right."
☐ ADVICE   ☐ SUPPORT

"It must be so hard to come home to a place where you don't feel welcome. I'm really sorry you're not getting any support from your foster mom."
☐ ADVICE   ☐ SUPPORT

"Of course you're broke—you spend all your money on hair, clothes, and eating out."
☐ ADVICE   ☐ SUPPORT

"I used to be broke. I know from my own experience that it can be hard to save money when you're not used to it. Does anyone have any good strategies?"
☐ ADVICE   ☐ SUPPORT

"I've found that when I'm really anxious or angry if I take 10 really deep breaths the feelings get a lot less intense."
☐ ADVICE   ☐ SUPPORT

"You've got an anger problem. You just need to deal with it."
☐ ADVICE   ☐ SUPPORT

Session 2: Building a Safe and Supportive Group

Griffin Kinard is having a lot of trouble coping with some big losses in his life. He needs support.

Digging Deep in My Soul
It's been hard to deal with the deaths in my life

By Griffin Kinard

Griffin Kinard

My family was two million miles short of perfect. My father hit and abused my siblings and me for no reason. My mother left as soon as she could.

Then, social services came and separated me from my siblings. The pain that I felt from watching first my mother, then my father, then my brothers leave me was unforgettable. I felt betrayed by my own people. It just killed me to see my family torn away one by one.

After a few foster homes and a hospital I was placed at a residential treatment center, where I stayed for the next nine years. It was pure hell.

I thought the abuse and the separations were enough mental testing for one person. Then the people close to me started leaving me for good.

Rushing My Own Death

When I was 9, my father went from being a man of strength to a man who needed to be pushed around in a wheelchair. He died of AIDS.

After my father died, I became reckless. I acted like nothing mattered. Looking back, I see now that I was rushing my own death. I could not bear the thought of being alive.

I started to go off on my own all the time. I was so sad that I was nobody's friend, and that my family did nothing but mess with me.

Eventually, I thought that killing myself was the answer. I tried to kill myself over and over again, but I failed each and every time. I think that part of me wanted to live.

I wasn't crazy. I was just too small to have experienced all that abuse, my mother disappearing and my father dying.

A Good Knight Sleeps

It took me years of spazzing out to move on. Finally, I did. I calmed down a lot. But the fight wasn't over yet.

When I was 16, I was in class when my social worker came and got me and took me to her office. She told me, "Griffin, your brother was shot." I was not shocked to hear the news because my brother had been shot before.

So I replied, "OK, is he in the hospital? Can I see him?"

"No, Griffin. Your brother was shot and killed."

The feelings that came over me I cannot explain.

My social worker asked me if I was all right.

"Yeah, I'm fine," I told her. Then I walked out of her office, only to see a door with a glass window. I punched the glass, but was still not fine. I could not get what she said out of my head. I could not grasp the truth. I repeated to myself, "My brother is not dead."

Pure Sadness and Anger

I arrived outside with tears in my eyes and blood dripping from my right hand. I started walking toward the busy street (not knowing why) but a voice in my head stopped me. It reminded me that people looked up to me.

That made me stop and think about a few things. Like, why is it that I cause harm to myself every time something devastating happens to me?

The last time I saw my brother he was cold like an iceberg. I was convinced my brother no longer had a soul. I felt nothing but pure sadness and anger. I did not see the point of living anymore.

That night after burying my brother, I thought to myself, "I am a knight and so was my brother. A knight is someone who plays the game down to the last dollar. He doesn't give up. Once he's in, he's in."

People always told me that I was a bright kid and that I could go far. I didn't believe their words at the time. But remembering my brother in his coffin, I really understood that life was short and I needed to make the most of mine.

Another Loss

Soon I was moved to a group home, where too many things happened. But the good part was I got a mentor who came to see me damn near every weekend.

We were real cool. He was white, I was black. It looked like opposites do attract. We went to the movies every weekend. Holidays we spent at his place. It was awesome and I was really enjoying it, but like all good things, it came to an end.

It was two weeks before Thanksgiving that I last saw Dale. A week later I walked into the group home and sat down to watch some television when the supervisor called me down to his office. He told me that my mentor had passed.

I didn't know what to do or say. I just cried tears of confusion. I thought, "Just a week ago we were making plans for Thanksgiving, and his family is making plans to bury him now?"

The Light in Death

It is very hard to find light when life gives you nothing but chaos and devastating situations. Losing my mentor and my family, I wanted to break down, give up. I had feelings I could no longer explain. I did not express my feelings to anybody. They were too raw.

To get through it I had to dig deep into my soul. When I got some time alone I was able to sit back and look at my life. I wrote a poem about someone dying and speaking their last words to their loved one, telling them that they love them no matter what.

Finding out that I could put my emotions on paper made me feel tough and ready for what the world threw at me. Soon I learned how to channel my feelings into poetry to the point that now the pen and the pad are my two best friends.

'Embrace Your Future'

Today, I write a poem for damn near every situation I

go through. Writing all that sadness and painful madness down has made those feelings just part of my past.

Now I remind myself, "Death is just death, not something to tear you apart. It's what we all wish for—peace and quiet." My time will come, but for now I try to enjoy everything life throws at me and to stay focused on the long run.

I tell myself, "Keep your mother-loving head up. Be proud of your past, accept your present, and embrace your future." I can keep the ones I lost in mind, but I must move on with my life.

Closing Reflection

▶ What did you learn about effective ways to communicate support without giving advice? Why might that be important in our workshop?

▶ What's comfortable to you as far as exposing yourself to the group? What do you have to gain from sharing in the group? What are the risks of sharing?

▶ How do you feel about the guidelines the group came up with today?

▶ Do you have any other questions about today's session?

Session 3

Introducing the Tools

Goals

- You'll have a solid understanding of the difference between **making a change** and **managing a transition**.

- You'll also reflect on a major change from your own past, and analyze the transition you went through when this change happened—and how you ultimately managed to handle things.

- You'll learn how tools—like talking with friends or mentors, reading, writing in a journal, prayer or mediation—can help you manage personal transitions.

- You'll learn about the different categories of tools.

- You'll identify the tools you already use, and the ones you'd like to use.

Change vs. Transition

In the Transitions workshop, we talk about change as something that happens outside of yourself, that you usually can't control. Change prompts a transition *inside of us* as we try to cope and adapt to new circumstances.

In the left-hand column, copy down several changes you've been through in your life. Then, in the right-hand column, describe the emotional transition you went through as you moved through that change. The first one is an example.

Session 3: Introducing the Tools

Changes in My Life	My Process of Transition
Things that **happened** (outside of you) What happened?	How you **reacted** and adapted to the change What kinds of emotions did you go through as part of your transition? How did you cope?
CHANGE: *Moved to a new school in fifth grade*	**TRANSITION:** *Felt angry, nervous and scared. I was fighting a lot. Then I got sent to the school social worker, who was nice. It made me feel relieved to have someone to talk to. I also made a few new friends. I started to feel calmer and safe.*
CHANGE:	**TRANSITION:**
CHANGE:	**TRANSITION:**
CHANGE:	**TRANSITION:**

Remembering to notice our strengths can really help when we're going through difficult experiences. Hattie tried to do exactly that as a way of helping herself cope with hard times.

Flipping the Script
How I stopped putting myself down

(Excerpted from Hattie's Transitions diary)

March 23

My constant self-criticism is not only crippling my self-esteem but also damaging my ability to try new things.

This week, I wrote some more about how I put myself down. This time, I wrote down some of the terrible criticisms I heard as a child, like: Why you sitting here talking to the quiet b-tch?" and "I can't even sit next to her. Yo, shorty a straight weirdo."

I was shocked to remember that a girl in my class had the audacity to talk about me like that to my face. But writing down those insults surprised me because my feelings were less intense than I thought they would be, which was good. I even reread what I wrote, which I never do.

My journal writing left me in such good

spirits that I decided on the first action I would take to change: I decided that for the rest of the week, I'd tell myself good things anytime something negative happened. It worked—somewhat. If I started criticizing myself, I was able to stop and tell myself good things.

The problem was, I didn't believe a word that was coming out of my mouth. I truly felt like a compulsive liar. Despite telling myself all these good things, I still felt incompetent, deep down. But I think that I need to program my first thought to be positive, and eventually my feelings about myself might catch up.

April 6

Continuing with my theme of telling myself positive things, I planned this week to put Post-Its on my mirror with my positive characteristics written on each. That way, I'll wake up with good feelings about myself, and I'll be able to study my positive qualities. I also wrote an on-the-go list of my positive qualities in my journal so I'd always have it with me.

The list included: introspective, intelligent, considerate, understanding, timid, intuitive, intricate, broad-minded, caring, and able to disregard my emotions during times of stress.

April 13

This week I chose to write a story about a time in my life when I used all the positive characteristics I'd posted on my mirror. The story was a way to remind myself of my strength.

Here's what I wrote:

"When I was home with my mom, she refused to talk to me. In fact, she refused to talk to any of her family. (She has schizophrenia and was addicted to crack for years). Everyone else left her alone and ignored her crying.

"Although I was only 12, I was intelligent and intuitive enough to realize that my mom wasn't OK and needed help expressing herself. So instead of going to school, I was considerate and sensitive of her feelings—I stayed home with her every day.

"I wasn't sad to miss school. When I was younger, going to school was painful because I had only two outfits, my skin looked horrible, and my mom would mess up my hair. So you can imagine how much I got teased. (I am amazed I go to school today).

"That year I stayed home I was patient. I knew of my mom's violent nature, so I waited and eventually she opened up to me. She told me how she felt watched, and she pulled the blinds down. She told me that a boyfriend she'd had when she was 10 hypnotized her and was now having her watched.

She claimed my father was in on it, too.

"As far-fetched as her story was, I listened and did not interrupt. The story was unreal, but her pain was not. The situation made me feel strong yet scared. It was good that my mom had me to turn to, but who did I have?

"Soon after that, I was placed in foster care. I am involved with my family but remain detached emotionally so I am able to live and not let their needs consume me. I still visit them, to show them my loyalty and let them know that they are irreplaceable."

Writing all of this down, I reminded myself of my strength and resilience. It was good to remember that there are reasons I have trouble feeling positive about my life, but also that the worst times are behind me.

Types of Tools

Here are the five major types of transitions tools, along with a few examples of each tool. Can you think of more examples?

1. Seeking Information
Reading, talking to people, taking a class, or searching the Web to find out more about the issue you're facing.

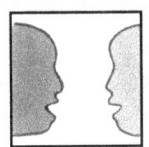

2. Social Support
Figuring out who could be helpful to you, and reaching out to them for support. (For example, talking to a friend, a family member or a trusted teacher or counselor, connecting with others who have been through a similar situation, joining a new team, group, or club.)

3. Reflection and Experimentation
Reflection: Thinking deeply about the issues you're facing and exploring how you really feel. (For example, journaling, writing about a past experience, or going to therapy.)

Experimentation: Trying something different from what you normally do and seeing how it makes you feel. (For example, speaking up in class instead of keeping your head down.)

4. Rituals and Ceremonies
Ritual: An activity you do regularly that helps you feel comfortable or calm. (For example, a hot bath every Saturday morning, or meditating before you go to bed).

Ceremony: An activity that symbolizes a change you're making or want to make. (For example, writing a goodbye letter to someone you've lost, and then burying it.)

5. Rewards and Recognition
Taking the time to acknowledge your accomplishments, and doing something nice for yourself. (For example, writing down one positive thing about yourself every day, or buying yourself a special treat when you've reached a new goal or are going through a difficult time.)

Session 3: Introducing the Tools

Tools in Action

Type of Tool: Seeking Information. Example: Read a book
Type of Tool: Ritual. Example: Writing in my diary

"I read a book called Path Finder about finding direction in your life. Once I finish reading a passage in the book, I write a progress note in my diary, so when I'm feeling down, I can look back and smile because I see how much I've grown over the months." **—Erica**

Type of Tool: Social Support.
Example: Help from teachers and social workers

"With my future transition—changing schools—I used social support by figuring out that my teacher and social worker would be helpful, but my family would not. I feel more in control of what's happening because I'm choosing who I want to share this transition with me. I feel a little less likely to fall to pieces because so many people are telling me so many things."
—Natasha

Type of Tool: Reflection. Example: Writing down my inner thoughts

"Since going to my new foster home, I haven't really felt comfortable talking to my foster mom, so as an alternative, I write to her to express myself. Simple situations angered me, so to avoid having an outburst at her, I started writing what I felt. I don't know how she interpreted it, but it felt good for me to express my inner thoughts." **—Hattie**

Type of Tool: Social Support. Example: Help from a mentor
Type of Tool: Reflection. Example: Thinking about important questions

"My mentor wrote down some questions for me to answer about how I worry so much and how that relates to me not being able to trust certain friends. In thinking about the questions, I learned that one reason I worry so much about this is that I haven't had healthy boundaries with my friends in the past." **—Michael**

Type of Tool: Reflection. Example: Writing out feelings

"Once I have dealt with an issue, I write about it as a state of closure. It's like writing away my past history to move on to a better future." **—Erica**

Type of Tool: Experimenting with Behavior.
Example: Opened up to my peers

"During my transition into foster care, I experimented with expressing my feelings and conversing with my peers. Before, I was quiet, but it was beautiful talking to people with similar situations. They didn't judge or criticize. Instead, they just let me express myself clearly and I felt free from the secrets that I'd held close for years." —Hattie

Type of Tool: Experimenting with Behavior.
Example: Didn't scream and shout

"When I changed foster homes, I wanted to scream and shout and be upset, but I didn't allow myself to. I think that this helped me a lot in the long run because I held it together for myself and it made me feel OK for a while." —Natasha

Type of Tool: Experimenting with Behavior. Example: I tried to act happy
Experiments sometimes give results different from what we expected, but we still learn!

"It didn't really work because I tried to act like I was happy, but I really wasn't and usually I would be pissed off and do dumb things because I was just acting cool rather than trying to address the struggles I was going through inside. I realized that wasn't a good solution, because I was still upset."
—Cynthia

Type of Tool: Experimenting with Behavior. Example: I tried to act macho

"When I moved to a new group home, I tried to act all macho but I didn't like the false persona it gave me. I realized it was important to me to be true to who I am, and if I could do that, I'd feel better about myself."
—Miguel

Type of Tool: Rewards and Recognition.
Example: Creating comfort

"I decided to surround myself with things that remind me of good times to make me feel comfortable and peaceful." —Michael

Type of Tool: Rewards and Recognition.
Example: Celebrate my positive qualities

"I put sticky notes on my mirror with my positive characteristics written on them – one for each note. That way, I'll wake up every morning with good feelings about myself, and I'll be able to study my positive qualities."
—Hattie

Session 3: Introducing the Tools

My Personal Tool Bank

Here are the same categories of tools from the Cheat Sheet on p. 115. In this Tool Bank, you are going to write down all the tools. You get to decide which ones you want to try out during the workshop. You can add new tools to the list at any time.

Seeking Information	Social Support	Reflection and Experimentation	Rituals and Ceremonies	Rewards and Recognition

Closing Reflection

▶ Which category of tools do you tend to rely on when you're going through a difficult change?

▶ Which category do you not use much, but would like to try? Why?

▶ Two questions or things you learned today:

Session 4

Owning the Tools

Goals

- You will become more familiar with Transitions tools and categories of tools.

- You'll construct your own personalized toolbox and put some of your best tools in it.

Closing Reflection

Reflect on the experience of creating your personal toolbox:

▶ What strengths do you see in your collage?

▶ What challenges have you coped with?

▶ How does thinking about past transitions make you feel about working on a new transition in this group?

Session 5

Stages of Transition—Letting Go

Goals

- You'll understand the emotions often associated with Letting Go, and realize that most people share these emotions (including everyone in the group).

- You'll learn that letting go isn't something you do once and then never do again. Rather, "letting go" is something that we'll be doing all of our lives—as we experience each new change in our lives.

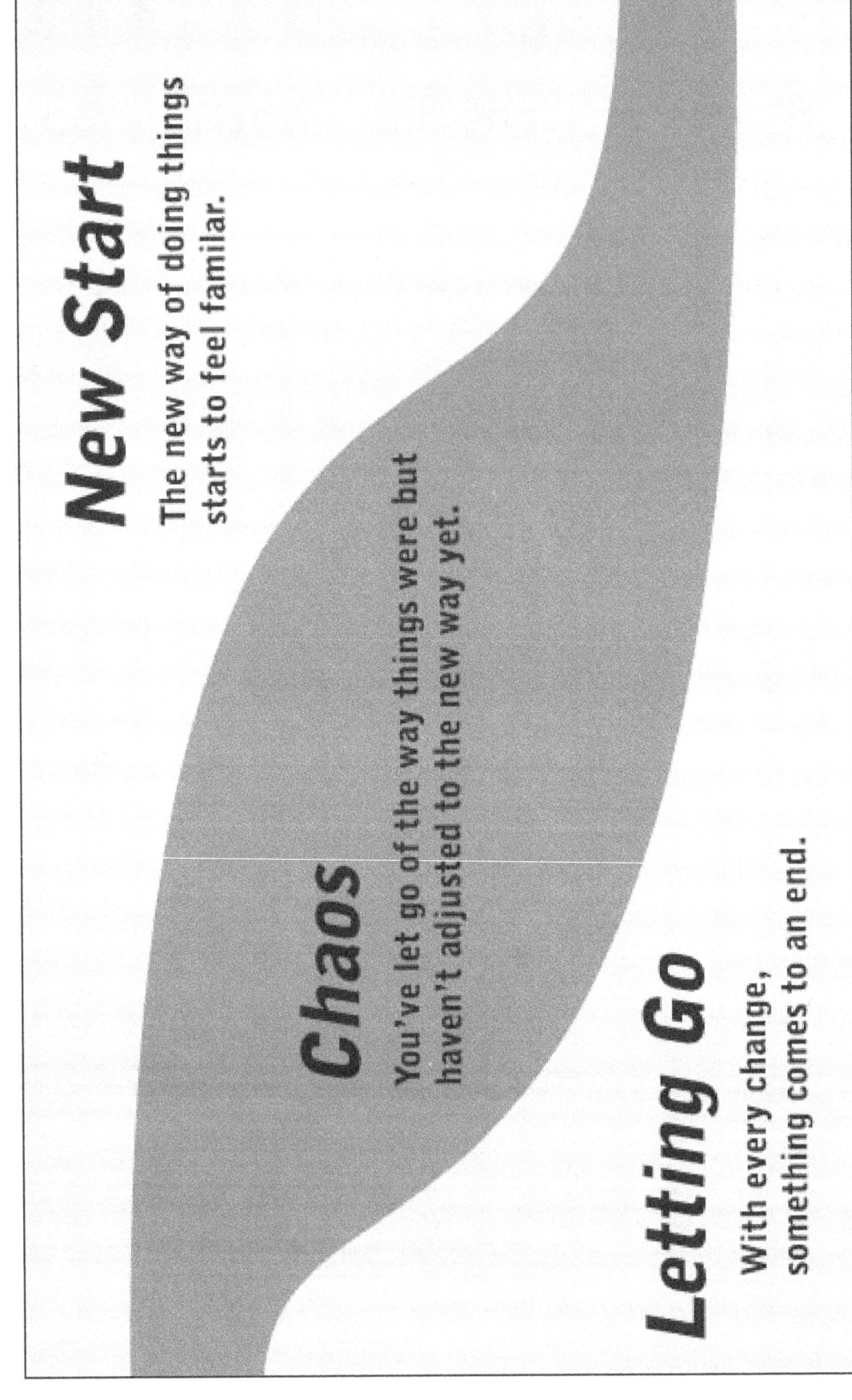

Session 5: Stages of Transition—Letting Go

Timeline of Your Life

Since we're going to be learning in this workshop how to achieve successful transitions throughout life, we need to think about the important events that have happened in our lives up to now, and some of the events that are still to come. By thinking about important events from the past, we'll start to see how we've handled changes up to now, and how we can use that information to handle changes in the future.

On the next page is a timeline where you can fill in the really important *changes* that have happened in your life. You don't have to have something written down for every year, and it's OK to have more than one thing written down for a certain year.

Use the scale on the left-hand side to measure how positive or negative the event was to you. You can rank positive events on a scale of 1-10, with 10 being the best or most positive and 1 being just a little positive. For the negative life events, -1 is the least negative and -10 is the worst. If you wish, you can also add in future events that you expect to happen, like aging out of foster care, graduating from high school/college, career, family plans, etc. You will not have to share this timeline with the group.

After you've written everything you want to include on the timeline, connect all the dots. Then answer the questions on the following page, which will ask you to reflect on the changes you've identified.

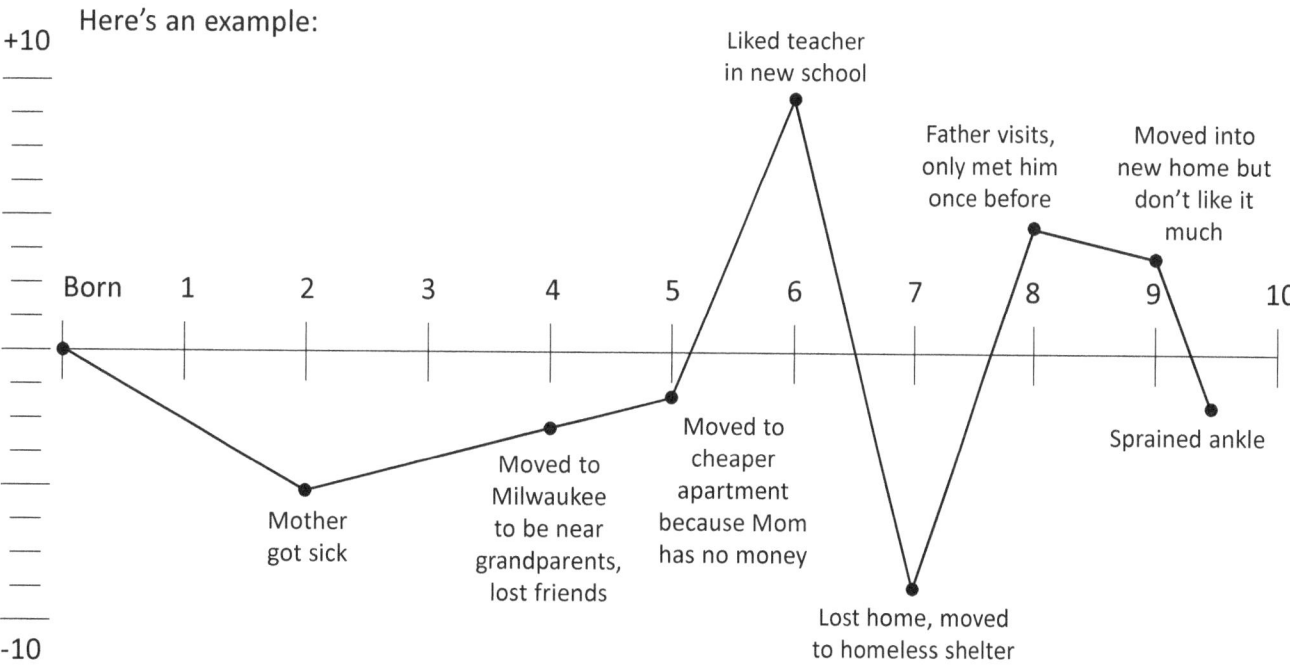

49

Timeline of Important Changes in My Life

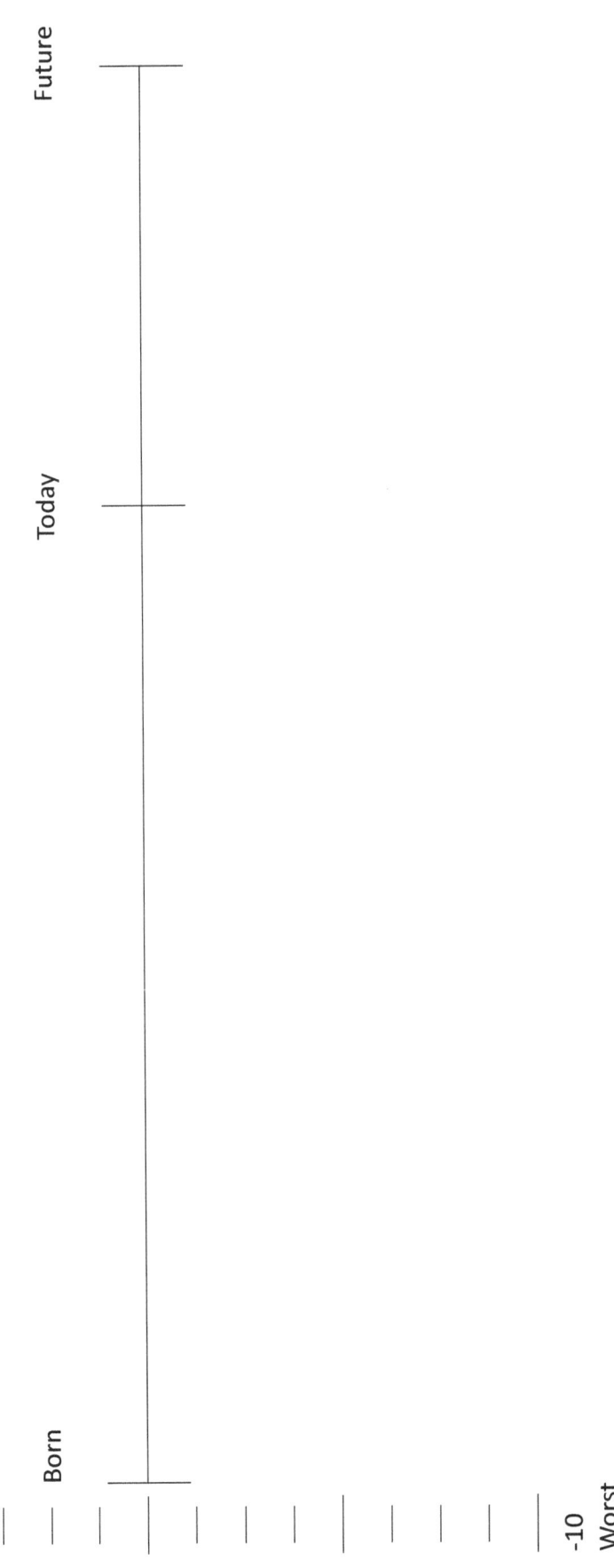

Timeline of My Life: Reflection

▶ Looking back at your timeline, what were some of the things you had to *let go of* during those changes in your life? How did you cope (positive or negative ways)? Do you feel like you were able to acknowledge what you were losing at the time? What other tools might have helped you work through Letting Go?

▶ Do any of the changes from your timeline still affect you? How?

Closing Reflection

▶ Are you going through (or about to go through) any changes in your life right now in which you feel you're in the Letting Go stage? What is the change? What are you losing or letting go of?

▶ List two questions or comments you have about today's session:

Session 6

Stages of Transition—Chaos

Goals

- You will learn about the Chaos stage and the emotions associated with it.

- You will name and describe strategies and tools that will help you cope with the Chaos stage.

Reflecting on Chaos

Sometimes the chaos stage can feel as though you've been dropped into the wilderness: a completely new environment that you aren't prepared for. But even in times of chaos, we all have certain strengths to draw upon to help us survive.

Think back to Hattie Rice, who wrote in her Transitions diary about the year she spent at home taking care of her mother. Hattie was always putting herself down and thinking negatively about herself, but after she reflected on that year, she realized she had some strengths that she hadn't realized before.

Think of a time you were in Chaos around a particular change in your life. What strengths did you draw on to help you through that period? What tools did you use?

Manning Up

I age out the same month my baby is born. Gulp.

By Christopher Guzman

Christopher Guzman

I was chilling at my godparents' house when I got the text from my girl Corrie. It had a picture attached that I didn't understand, so I texted her back, "wwwhhh-haaaaatttttt?" Her next text said, "Negative is the straight line; positive is the plus sign." I looked back at the picture: a plastic stick with a plus sign.

I knew her period was late, but now it was real. I threw my phone in the air and laughed and yelled at the same time. I was scared but also amazed that I was bringing a life into the world. I couldn't believe this was happening to me.

We didn't intend to get pregnant, but I don't believe in abortion. I asked Corrie what she wanted to do, and she told me that she doesn't believe in abortion either. She said, "I'm going to leave it in; we're going to have a family."

So I'm going to be a father. I don't know much about what's going to happen, but I know I don't want to do what my father did—he left my family the day I was born. He just walked out and left a letter to my mom saying, "I'm not ready to be a father to three boys. PEACE." He moved to Puerto Rico to make a whole new foundation, including starting another family. That hurt. He didn't see me before he left, but it still feels like a personal rejection.

Me as a Father

I feel like a kid in a kid's body, partly because I'm short, and also because I'm only 20 and haven't even aged out of care yet. I need a job and a place to live. I don't really feel ready to be a father. I feel more stress than ever imagining what it will be like when the baby is born. I know it's going to be stressful when the baby wakes up early in the morning, needs changing, needs feeding. It's hard for me to deal with new things that I'm not used to. Knowing that I'm not ready makes it more difficult to hear family members, friends and associates say, "You're not ready! How are you going to pay for this? Where are you going to live?" It's too much.

I need to get a job to support my child. I need money for rent and health insurance and to take the baby to the hospital if it's sick, to buy baby food and clothes. There's so much I don't know about a baby, but I do know that responsibility comes first.

To be a father, I have to change my life and become a better person because I've been a knucklehead. I've been hanging around with my friends—smoking, drinking, partying, doing what normal teenagers do. In August my life will change completely: the baby is due, and I turn 21 and age out of care.

I'd like to worry less, but I have more to worry about than ever. Becoming a father is the hardest and scariest thing that I can think of besides going to war.

How Do I Learn This Stuff?

I didn't have a father to look up to who could understand what I was going through. I had role models and father figures, but no one can replace a father growing up. I always wanted what someone else had because there was no one to buy things for me or take me to the movies. Even after I turned 18, I still missed having a father. I wish that I'd had a father to talk to when I needed some advice about things that I don't know—including being a father!

I don't want my child growing up like I did. That's why I'm going to give my baby what my father didn't give to me: guidance, encouragement, strength, hope, and the most important, love.

Taking Care of Others

I've made a good start by going with Corrie to her doctor's appointments. The day that I went to the first ultrasound was the happiest day ever. I saw my baby for the first time as an embryo. I was proud of myself for playing the role and stepping up.

Corrie was in a lot of pain during the ultrasound. I was holding her hand throughout it. I told her "Baby, you're OK, everything's going to be OK," letting her know that we're in this together. I felt like a husband holding his wife through the pain and struggles.

While the nurse was taking the pictures of the baby I was asking her very important questions about the baby, but she ignored me! I was shocked. Corrie asked a question and the nurse answered her. I got very offended.

I wanted to smack fire out of the nurse. But I calmed down. I was proud of holding my temper because it showed me that I'm not quitting for anything. I'm already doing more than my father ever did. I got a book about pregnancy and I've been reading about the growth of the baby, how it looks, how much it should weigh, and things like that.

Afterward, I was walking home just looking at the picture of the baby I'd taken on my phone and I started crying again. I cried every emotion, but mostly I was scared about the responsibility and happy because I'm bringing another human being into this world.

Me and Corrie

Corrie and I have a good connection, but things have changed since we found out about the baby. We barely speak to each other or see each other anymore. I call her and we only talk about the baby and what we're going to do and stuff. We used to joke around more. Things are more serious now, not fun.

We're losing a part of each other because of the baby. We're losing love because things aren't the way they used to be. She's tired and nauseous and I've been tired and worried about where we're going to live. I need help with everything.

We're going to be One no matter what, but now we're not One, feelings-wise. I told her that I was worried that we were drifting apart, that we barely kiss or converse. She said, "Sorry that it's happening like this; it will get better." I said, "Whatever."

I wonder how it would be if we were not having a baby. Sometimes I wonder if she would have broken up with me by now. She was on me to get a job even before she got pregnant.

Family

Corrie's dad died when she was young, and she's very close to her mother. She has a sister who also had a baby last year. Corrie's mother and cousins and aunts and grandmother fight over who gets to babysit that baby.

I wish I had a mother like that and I'm glad for the support. But sometimes it seems like I have to prove myself to Corrie's mother. I look for jobs and apartments every day, but Corrie and her mother act like I'm not trying hard enough. They'll ask, "Well, why didn't you do this or do that?" It makes me feel like they don't believe me, like they're asking for proof of what I do all day.

Corrie doesn't like any of the names I've picked for the baby. I wanted my friend to be the godmother, but Corrie chose someone else. I want my kid to eat chicken and meat, and Corrie's already decided the baby will be a vegetarian.

An apartment below her mother's apartment might become available, and if we live there, I know her mother will be making a lot of the decisions about the baby. I worry that if I don't get a job or get into school or get a place to live soon that they'll only treat me like the baby-father, not the father.

But I want to be the father. I want to wake up every day and strive to provide for my child. I've accepted that this baby is what matters most now, more than all of my fears and the obstacles in my past.

Even though I don't have parents, I have people who will help. My godparents will be like grandparents. I know that they will help me in any way possible. They took me in after I left from a group home upstate and accepted me into the family.

I'm also glad to have my friends Kalid, Marc, and Dre, even though Dre moved to Texas last year. He and I always joked around calling each other "son" and "my child." When I told him Corrie was pregnant, he said "Wow, I'm going to become a grandfather," and we both laughed. I asked all three of those guys to be godfather to my baby. They said that they were happy to be a part of the baby's life and that they'd be there for us 100 percent.

August

I turn 21 and age out on August 5. What turning 21 means is losing all the money I got for school, for clothes, food, housing, transportation, haircuts, everything. My baby is due August 22, and I have to be there to take care of it. I want my baby to have birth parents, not be part of the system.

Now my responsibility is to become a good father. I'm getting up every day to look for jobs and internships and colleges that will accept a special education diploma (which is really a certificate that says I completed high school). I also study on my own time just to stay on track with my education.

I'm going to take a fatherhood class to prepare me to become a successful father. I'm still afraid because we're in a recession, and how am I going to find a job if nobody's hiring? But even though it's hard, I won't stop trying because somebody is depending on me now to live a successful life.

Finding Our Way Through Chaos

1. What emotions does Chris experience when he first finds out he's going to be a father?

2. At what point in the story do you feel that Chris has moved from the Letting Go stage to the Chaos stage? Why?

3. Often, going through an emotional transition can trigger memories of another time when we felt the same difficult emotions we're feeling now. What are some of Chris's difficult moments in his struggle to prepare for fatherhood? What memories or emotions do those moments trigger?

4. What does Chris have to let go of to make this transition? Has he completely let go yet? How will he know when he's in the New Start stage?

5. If you were Chris's friend, what tools would you suggest he use to help him work on his transition at this stage? Try to think of at least five.

Session 6: Stages of Transition—Chaos

Closing Reflection

▶ Are you going through any transitions in your life right now in which you feel you are in the Chaos stage? What is the transition? What do you hope your New Start will be?

▶ Two things you learned from today's session, or questions you have.

Session 7

Stages of Transition—New Start

Goals

- You'll understand the characteristics, emotions, and tools that are often part of the New Start stage of transition.

- You'll understand the idea that New Start is not the same as an ending, because we tend to circle back through transitions – one change and transition leads to another (and change and transition are not always negative!).

- You'll think about some personal changes in your life that you might like to focus on in Part Two of the workshop.

- You'll reflect on how the first half of the workshop went and offer some positive affirmations to your fellow group members.

Cinderella's New Start?

We all know the story of how Cinderella suffered at the hands of her wicked stepmother and stepsisters after the death of her father. They put her to work as their servant and controlled her every move. Lucky for Cinderella, her fairy godmother waved her magic wand and transformed Cinderella into the belle of the ball. Just one look, and Prince Charming was in love. The couple got married—and supposedly lived happily ever after. A New Start for Cinderella!

Hmmmm. Happily ever after? Is that the same thing as *perfectly* ever after? Real life isn't perfect, as we all know, and being happy all the time isn't very realistic. Do you ever wonder what *really* happened to Cinderella after the wedding?

In this activity, your job is to imagine what happens after "The End" of that famous fairy tale. Remember, Cinderella is going through a drastic change—from poor, mistreated servant to wealthy, adored princess. To manage a successful transition, she'll have to go through all the stages we've learned about. These questions will help you think through what she's really facing. Then, you'll imagine a *realistic movie sequel* to the Cinderella story.

1. Even though this is a welcome change for Cinderella, we know that every transition involves letting go of something. What does Cinderella have to let go of? What feelings might that bring up?

2. How might she be feeling in the Chaos stage? What might she do to cope?

3. How will Cinderella know if she's made it to the New Start?

Session 7: Stages of Transition—New Start

4. What difficult memories from Cinderella's past might get in her way after she makes a new start?

Now, write your sequel here. How does Cinderella's life change after marrying Prince Charming? How does she get to a successful New Start?

Thinking About Your Transition

Over the second half of the workshop, you'll be using everything you've learned so far to work on a change in your own life. The change you pick can be something you've already spoken or written about in the group, or it could be one you haven't mentioned yet.

Because you'll stick with this change for the remainder of the workshop, we want you to take your time choosing it. Brainstorm several possible changes and write a little bit about each. Then we'll talk about the possibilities, and you'll have until our next session to think it over and make a decision about which change you want to pick.

A few things to keep in mind: The change should be something that you are still in Letting Go or Chaos on—something that you are still struggling with. Also, make sure that you pick something that you feel you will be able to work on for a sustained period of time, and that really matters to your life long-term.

1) List three changes that you could potentially work on for the rest of the workshop. These can be things you've already written or talked about, or something new. Describe each change, which stage of transition you think you're in, and why you'd like to work on it.

Change 1:

Change 2:

Change 3:

2) List any fears or concerns you have about tackling each of these transitions.

Change 1:

Change 2:

Change 3:

3) As we learned when we talked about Letting Go, every change, even a good change, means losing something else. Write down what you have lost or will lose if you make each change. What will you gain?

Change 1:

Change 2:

Change 3:

PART II
Transitions in Action

SESSIONS 8-16

You'll choose one transition from your own life that you'd like to work on. Each week, you'll pick a new tool to try. In the group, you'll report back on how it went, and get and give feedback to your fellow group members. The last session is a celebration or graduation ceremony.

Session 8

Identifying Your Change

Goals

- You'll choose a change to work on for the next few weeks, set goals, and get feedback from the group.

- You'll understand that change goes in cycles, and will continue throughout life.

- You'll understand that you don't have to reach every goal to have a successful transition.

- You'll appreciate the value and importance of self-discovery in the Transitions process. (The more you learn about yourself, the more control you will have over future transitions.)

- You'll learn how the past can affect your transitions and how to avoid getting stuck there.

Choosing Your Change

1. YOUR CHANGE: Please state the change you will work on for the next six weeks. (If this is not one of the changes you wrote about in the last session, make sure to describe it in detail, including what stage you think you're in now, what you will be losing, what concerns you have, and why you'd like to work on this change.)

The change I'm going to work on is:

2. GOALS FOR MY TRANSITION: Please write down a short, specific list of the goals you want to achieve with this transition. What are *specific* feelings you would like to understand better? What are *specific* behaviors you want to change or try out? What are *specific, reasonable* goals you want to aim for in the next few months?

Session 8: Identifying Your Change

Planning Your Transition

Now that you've chosen your change, it's time to start thinking about your plan for working through it. Today, we're going to read "School Daze," the story of how Natasha used this workshop and the tools to help her get through a big change: going to a new school.

This change brought up all kinds of difficult emotions and memories for Natasha. She tried some tools that worked, and others that didn't. In the end, Natasha was not sure if she really achieved the goal she made for herself at the beginning of the workshop. But going through the process, she did make positive progress (Natasha went on to college and is doing well, even though she still has her ups and downs).

As you read Natasha's story, keep your own chosen change in mind. Though your transition may be different than hers, notice the things she says that you connect with: feelings, actions, patterns, habits, etc.

Afterward, you'll think about the questions on p. 85 and discuss them with a partner. You should each take turns answering every question. It's OK to say that you are not comfortable answering a question or are not sure.

School Daze
I tried to change my old ways at a new school

By Natasha Santos

Natasha Santos

So there I was on the train to visit City-As-School for the first time. From what I'd been told, it was an alternative high school for people who don't feel comfortable in a traditional school setting. Translation: Some rinky-dink hole-in-the-wall manufactured to house academic misfits. But I was failing at my old school, so I didn't have much choice.

My mother's death, "growing pains," a creeping sense of failure and an inability to communicate what help I needed had all contributed to me not doing well in school.

In therapy, I was working out many of the painful feelings and events of my childhood that I'd tried to suppress for years. Dealing with awful feelings that I'd never dealt with before took its toll on my motivation and then my grades.

Sitting in the City-As auditorium, I told myself I was too smart for this. Sure I had failed, but I would do better. My mind began to change as I heard the assistant princi-

Session 8: Identifying Your Change

pal say something like, "It is your responsibility to take control of your education. We'll help you if that's what you want. The traditional public school system wasn't good enough for you so you sought out an alternative. You haven't been accepted yet, but you have made the first step."

Two weeks later I registered for classes. Unlike most schools, at City-As students get most of their credits through internships. For science credit, I started working at the Central Park Zoo.

I found my classes and internships engaging. I also liked that teachers didn't give much homework. But at the same time I felt—and still feel—that I hadn't been through a process of transition to really feeling like I could succeed in school and that I was on the right path to adulthood.

When I signed up for the Transitions workshop, I decided to focus on making that change. In the group, we tried specific activities (we called them "tools") that we thought would help us make a change in our lives, and we kept journals of our efforts. Here's my journal of my attempts to succeed in my new school and be in charge of my education and future.

Session 1

At my old school, Murrow, I didn't have too much trouble with the workload. My real problem was feeling disconnected—I felt like a loner.

When I first entered Murrow (as a sophomore, transferring from a smaller school) I wasn't brave enough to connect with other students. Then, as I felt more and more lonely, I didn't spend enough time actually at school to meet people. I've decided that at City-As I need to actually show up, and be brave enough to put myself out there. (Gulp.)

It's always been easier for me to connect with adults than with people my age, so for my first challenge, I decided to speak to teachers about the change I am trying to make and ask their advice about how to succeed.

I loved this tool! I got nothing but positivity from my teachers. When I asked my social studies teacher how I was doing he said, "Great, you're one of the most involved and mature people in my class."

And my English teacher seemed enraptured by my work. It was a nice break from Murrow where I was constantly avoiding teachers because I had cut their class and had work due. Perhaps my family was right—I just needed to leave Murrow and start fresh to succeed.

Session 2

One tool is to write letters to people you are or have been close to, even if you don't send them. I decided to write a letter to Murrow telling the school why I'm making this change, and saying good-bye. I decided to keep my letter short and sweet because I didn't want to cry or shout or go completely crazy. I wrote:

Session 8: Identifying Your Change

Dear Murrow,

I came to Murrow to get what I had always wanted: a place where I was welcomed and academically challenged. I also had always wanted to feel connected to school and the people there (maybe because I felt so disconnected in my foster home).

School had never been a problem for me in the past. I would never have been voted Ms. Popular, but I knew who I was through my academics. I was an overachiever. People called me weird and unique and smart.

That has been part of my persona since elementary school. My home life was always crazy, so school was the place that anchored me to a reality that I wanted. All of this was possible as long as I stayed the smart, dependable student. No matter what else I may have been, I was always that.

When I started failing in Murrow I could no longer identify myself as the achiever and the smart one. Smart ones didn't fail classes. Overachievers achieved with ease. I was still the weird one, but even that took on a kind of melancholy tilt.

Now I am going to try to find a new me in a new school.

Wish me luck,
Tasha

I think writing the letter helped me understand more of what had happened. But when I looked back at it a few weeks later, I didn't feel released: I felt upset and disappointed in Murrow and myself. I guess it was time to begin feeling some of the emotions I wouldn't let myself feel while I was still at Murrow.

Session 3

This week I decided to talk to some of the people who I thought were interesting and nice in my English class.

I expected it to be easy to work on my social skills and my feelings of belonging. But trying to make friends also brought up some feelings from my past that I didn't expect. In my other schools and foster homes I had always had trouble with fitting in and belonging. I was rejected by some of my former classmates and my former foster mother after I gave so much of myself.

Talking to my classmates, I noticed I was anxious about putting myself out there. I felt afraid that there was something wrong with me, something unlovable and unchangeable that made everyone run away and will make anyone new run away, too.

I did meet one guy named Jess who was real cool. He has blue hair and a constant nervous smile. He first caught my attention because he was good at math (I'm terrible at math). I decided to ask Jess for help (really I just copied his answers, but it was a start).

Now that I've talked to him, I have someone to call about homework and maybe become friends with.

I feel pretty proud that I was brave enough to put myself out there and try to get to know someone.

Session 4

I decided to speak to three new people a day at my school. I thought that talking to people would be just like a ritual, and would become more and more comfortable. But it went terribly. I found out just how big of a coward I am about meeting people. At best I would say, "Hi, how are you doing," to two people. At worst I would just smile and nod to everyone I saw.

I thought that I would become outgoing, the center of attention, just because I wanted to. I guess I'm more reserved than I knew. I feel pretty bad about the whole thing. I feel like I found out I am a big 'fraidy cat and that no one in my new school really wants to get to know me.

It reminded me of what happened at Murrow. Murrow seemed like the perfect climate for me at first. It was open and intellectual: there were hundreds of groups and cliques and tons of clubs to join. But instead of finding a way to join a single group, I became a loner and recluse. In a building with thousands of people, I was alone.

At other times, when I'd experienced this failure to connect, I'd never blamed it on myself. I'd blamed it on my foster mother, my social workers and the kids at my previous stupid narrow-minded school. But if it still happened in a place like Murrow, the only person I could really blame was myself, and that hurt. Trying to meet people at City-As, I wondered if it could happen again, and if something terrible was wrong with me.

After two weeks of trying, I decided I was putting myself out there more than I wanted to and it brought up too many old feelings of rejection that I don't want to deal with.

Session 5

In the workshop this week, I didn't talk about how hard my last two weeks were, and how I felt like giving up. I don't think anyone noticed, but I felt bad after the meeting. I felt like I was lying in a place where everyone had agreed to be as open and honest as possible.

For my tool this week I decided not to try anything that would require interacting with new people. Instead, I chose to write in my diary about my school life. It didn't go well. Some days I would open up my journal and think of all the things I should write, and other days I just would stare at it in its place on the headboard in my room.

Session 8: Identifying Your Change

In the end, I was too afraid to actually record what I had felt and experienced during the day. So I changed my tool. I took some time out each day to go bike riding. I've just learned to ride a bike (late bloomer) and I love this new ability of mine. While I'm riding I just have my thoughts and the feeling of riding through the wind. (Though I should also try to pay a little attention to the bike and the road—I fell off three times.) If I couldn't face my feelings, at least I could escape them for a while.

Session 6

The workshop is almost over, so I decided to hold a "Congratulations on Our Successful Transitions" luncheon. I planned on inviting all the participants in the workshop.

I made out invitations, but then I realized that I didn't feel all that successful, so celebrating didn't feel honest to me. In fact, I was feeling even more like I was only faking my transition. I didn't even try to do my tools during the last two weeks.

Looking Back

Later, looking over my transitions diary, I realized that this pattern is familiar to me: I tend to come out strong, then get scared and back away. I've been trying to be a person I'm not comfortable being and to enjoy experiences I can't really handle.

I realized that I want to take things slower, not expecting to make 10 new best friends in two weeks, but just to find one or two people to talk to about our classes, little things like that. I want to evaluate my goals and how to achieve them without overwhelming myself.

If I'm reasonable about what I expect from myself, I think I might accomplish much more. In fact, lately I've been feeling less overwhelmed and isolated at school. I'm participating in my classes, my grades are good, and I'm slowly meeting my classmates. I might actually have some good experiences in high school after all.

Even though I don't yet feel connected to my school and fully responsible for my education and life, I think the tools have helped me better understand the process of transition.

Before, I saw changes as things that happen to you whether you're ready or not. I didn't see changes as opening up the possibility of internal development. And I've always been afraid that I don't have what it takes to make any change, whatever it is.

I realize now that my life will be a continuing cycle of transitions, and that the changes I need to make can help me grow, not leave me stuck further and further behind. I also see that I try to make changes happen too quickly. Now I see that I can slow down. That makes me feel more confident in my ability to evolve and grow.

Session 8: Identifying Your Change

Partner Questions for School Daze

Natasha talks about emotions she experienced while going through the Transitions workshop. Write down some of the emotions she describes. Which of those feelings do you share with Natasha, in terms of going through a transition in your life?

Did all of Natasha's tools work? Why do you think she had success with some tools and not others?

What were some of the things that got in Natasha's way? What are some of the things you think might interfere with making your own change and managing that transition?

What did Natasha get out of the program, even if she didn't achieve exactly the "success" she wanted?

What would success look like to you with your own transition? If you don't achieve the goal you set for yourself at the beginning, will you still consider yourself successful? Why/why not? Is it possible to achieve success even if you don't reach your goal in the workshop? What might that look like?

Closing Reflection

▶ How did reading Natasha's Transitions diary help you think about ways to approach your own process of transition? Did you get any ideas from the way she went about it?

▶ What concerns or questions do you have going forward?

Session 9

Tools That Will Work for Me

Goals

- You'll set goals and make a plan for using tools to reach them!

- You'll explore and review the benefits of sharing with the group, and think about how to set appropriate boundaries for your own sharing.

Personal Ground Rules

As we've seen already, the workshop can sometimes make us feel great. Other times it can raise difficult emotions that we don't know how to deal with. The following list can help you focus on issues that may come up for you as we proceed through the second half of the transitions workshop. We've already created some ground rules for the group. After you become conscious of how you respond to difficult emotions, you can create some personal ground rules, to help yourself deal with those difficult moments if they arise.

Check off any of the sentences that apply to you. Feel free to add others:

- ☐ I usually go further than I'm really comfortable going and then feel burnt out.
- ☐ I often put too much pressure on myself to succeed, and wind up feeling like I'm failing.
- ☐ I can feel so afraid of trying, that I don't try at all.
- ☐ I know I'll beat myself up for not using my tools right.
- ☐ I'm afraid this workshop will bring up strong emotions and I'll freak out.
- ☐ I'm afraid I'll stir up bad feelings and then be all alone with them.
- ☐ When things get hard, I withdraw and go through the motions without paying attention to what I'm really feeling or really letting people know what I'm struggling with.
- ☐ When things get hard I'm afraid I'll skip sessions without paying attention to what I'm struggling with.
- ☐ I'm afraid I'll quit when I get uncomfortable.
- ☐ _____
- ☐ _____
- ☐ _____
- ☐ _____

Adapted from The Courage to Heal Workbook by Laura Davis

Session 9: Tools That Will Work for Me

Now use the issues you've identified as the basis for your ground rules.

For example, if you push yourself too hard and then feel burnt out, you might want to limit the amount of time you'll devote to using your tools. If you're so afraid of trying that you never start, you might want to give yourself a specific time to devote to using your tools each week, even if you hate every minute and your efforts feel like a total flop.

Don't write down any ground rules that feel forced. Your ground rules should be things that you think will work for you.

Take a few minutes to write down some beginning ground rules here:

Setting Boundaries

This exercise is for your eyes only. If, after you do the exercise, you've written down things that you don't want to have down on paper, feel free to cross them out or erase them.

We already know from reading Natasha's Transitions diary that the process can raise a lot of different emotions. So it can be helpful to think about what you do want to share and what you don't want to share with others. Maybe we don't want to bring up certain memories from our past. But we can still share other memories. Or we can share our current struggles and feelings. Writing down the things we definitely *don't* want to share can free us up to see all the parts of ourselves that we do want to bring to the group.

Of course, our feelings can change over time. This is just a place to start.

Below, finish the following prompts with whatever comes to mind.

Things I don't want to share are:

Things I do want to share are:

Things I might want to share are:

Choosing a Tool

Weekly Assignment – Session 9

1. Right now I feel _____ about my transition.

2. One thing I am thinking about (struggling with, would like to build on) regarding my transition is:

3. What tool will you use this week?
Directions: Look through your toolbox and back at your Personal Tool Bank on p. 43 and the Tools Cheat Sheet on p. 115. Pick one tool and write it down exactly.

I will use:

4. Explain how exactly you plan to use this tool.
Directions: Describe what you plan to do. For example, if you are going to set a daily ritual, what will the ritual be? Your plans should feel challenging but achievable.

I plan to:

5. What worries or concerns do you have about trying this tool? How can you address them?

TRANSITIONS JOURNAL

Closing Reflection – Session 9

▶ Things I got from the group today:

▶ Questions I have right now:

Sessions 10-15

Using the Tools

Goals

- You will try a range of tools for managing your transition and decide which ones worked best.

- You will continue working on building trust and supportive communication skills as you share your progress with the group.

Reporting Back – Session 10

Today's Date: _____

The tool I tried last week was...
(In addition to naming the tool, describe exactly what you actually did. This might be different from what you had planned to do last week.)

How did it go? Was it helpful or not helpful? Why?

If you did not use your tool the way you thought you were going to, explain why.

*Something from my past that's been getting in my way is *(optional):

Something I learned or discovered about myself this week was...

Sessions 10-15: Using the Tools

Choosing a Tool – Session 10

1. Right now I feel _____ about my transition.

2. One thing I am thinking about (struggling with, would like to build on) regarding my transition is:

3. **What tool will you use this week?**
Directions: Look through your toolbox and back at your Personal Tool Bank on p. 43 and the Tools Cheat Sheet on p. 115. Pick one tool and write it down exactly.

I will use:

4. **Explain how exactly you plan to use this tool.**
Directions: Describe what you plan to do. For example, if you are going to set a daily ritual, what will the ritual be? Your plans should feel challenging but achievable.

I plan to:

5. What worries or concerns do you have about trying this tool? How can you address them?

Closing Reflection – Session 10

▶ **Things I got from the group today:**

▶ **Questions I have right now:**

Sessions 10-15: Using the Tools

Reporting Back – Session 11

Today's Date: _____

The tool I tried last week was...
(In addition to naming the tool, describe exactly what you actually did. This might be different from what you had planned to do last week.)

How did it go? Was it helpful or not helpful? Why?

If you did not use your tool the way you thought you were going to, explain why.

*Something from my past that's been getting in my way is *(optional):

Something I learned or discovered about myself this week was...

Choosing a Tool – Session 11

1. Right now I feel _____ about my transition.

2. One thing I am thinking about (struggling with, would like to build on) regarding my transition is:

3. What tool will you use this week?
Directions: Look through your toolbox and back at your Personal Tool Bank on p. 43 and the Tools Cheat Sheet on p. 115. Pick one tool and write it down exactly.

I will use:

4. Explain how exactly you plan to use this tool.
Directions: Describe what you plan to do. For example, if you are going to set a daily ritual, what will the ritual be? Your plans should feel challenging but achievable.

I plan to:

5. What worries or concerns do you have about trying this tool? How can you address them?

Closing Reflection – Session 11

▶ **Things I got from the group today:**

▶ **Questions I have right now:**

Reporting Back – Session 12

Today's Date: _____

The tool I tried last week was...
(In addition to naming the tool, describe exactly what you actually did. This might be different from what you had planned to do last week.)

How did it go? Was it helpful or not helpful? Why?

If you did not use your tool the way you thought you were going to, explain why.

*Something from my past that's been getting in my way is *(optional):

Something I learned or discovered about myself this week was...

Choosing a Tool – Session 12

1. Right now I feel _____ about my transition.

2. One thing I am thinking about (struggling with, would like to build on) regarding my transition is:

3. **What tool will you use this week?**
Directions: Look through your toolbox and back at your Personal Tool Bank on p. 43 and the Tools Cheat Sheet on p. 115. Pick one tool and write it down exactly.

I will use:

4. **Explain how exactly you plan to use this tool.**
Directions: Describe what you plan to do. For example, if you are going to set a daily ritual, what will the ritual be? Your plans should feel challenging but achievable.

I plan to:

5. What worries or concerns do you have about trying this tool? How can you address them?

Closing Reflection – Session 12

▶ Things I got from the group today:

▶ Questions I have right now:

Sessions 10-15: Using the Tools

Reporting Back – Session 13

Today's Date: _____

The tool I tried last week was...
(In addition to naming the tool, describe exactly what you actually did. This might be different from what you had planned to do last week.)

How did it go? Was it helpful or not helpful? Why?

If you did not use your tool the way you thought you were going to, explain why.

*Something from my past that's been getting in my way is *(optional):

Something I learned or discovered about myself this week was...

Choosing a Tool – Session 13

1. Right now I feel _____ about my transition.

2. One thing I am thinking about (struggling with, would like to build on) regarding my transition is:

3. What tool will you use this week?
Directions: Look through your toolbox and back at your Personal Tool Bank on p. 43 and the Tools Cheat Sheet on p. 115. Pick one tool and write it down exactly.

I will use:

4. Explain how exactly you plan to use this tool.
Directions: Describe what you plan to do. For example, if you are going to set a daily ritual, what will the ritual be? Your plans should feel challenging but achievable.

I plan to:

5. What worries or concerns do you have about trying this tool? How can you address them?

Closing Reflection – Session 13

▶ **Things I got from the group today:**

▶ **Questions I have right now:**

Reporting Back – Session 14

Today's Date: _____

The tool I tried last week was...
(In addition to naming the tool, describe exactly what you actually did. This might be different from what you had planned to do last week.)

How did it go? Was it helpful or not helpful? Why?

If you did not use your tool the way you thought you were going to, explain why.

*Something from my past that's been getting in my way is *(optional):

Something I learned or discovered about myself this week was...

Sessions 10-15: Using the Tools

Choosing a Tool – Session 14

1. Right now I feel _____ about my transition.

2. One thing I am thinking about (struggling with, would like to build on) regarding my transition is:

3. **What tool will you use this week?**
Directions: Look through your toolbox and back at your Personal Tool Bank on p. 43 and the Tools Cheat Sheet on p. 115. Pick one tool and write it down exactly.

I will use:

4. **Explain how exactly you plan to use this tool.**
Directions: Describe what you plan to do. For example, if you are going to set a daily ritual, what will the ritual be? Your plans should feel challenging but achievable.

I plan to:

5. What worries or concerns do you have about trying this tool? How can you address them?

Closing Reflection – Session 14

▶ **Things I got from the group today:**

▶ **Questions I have right now:**

Sessions 10-15: Using the Tools

Reporting Back – Session 15

Today's Date: _____

The tool I tried last week was...
(In addition to naming the tool, describe exactly what you actually did. This might be different from what you had planned to do last week.)

How did it go? Was it helpful or not helpful? Why?

If you did not use your tool the way you thought you were going to, explain why.

*Something from my past that's been getting in my way is *(optional):

Something I learned or discovered about myself this week was...

Closing Reflection – Session 15

▶ Things I got from the group today:

▶ Questions I have right now:

Session 16

Celebrate!

Use this page to write down a few things you're proud of, things you've learned that you'd like to remember, or any other thoughts about the end of the workshop.

APPENDIX

CHEAT SHEETS
JOURNALS

Transitions Tools Cheat Sheet

 Rituals and Ceremonies

- Listening to music
- Going to church
- Volunteering regularly
- Meditating
- Praying
- Doing your hair/makeup
- Exercising
- Painting or other creative activity
- Reading about common rituals and ceremonies in different cultures and adapting one to your needs
- Making up your own ceremony

 Social Support

- Talking to a therapist/counselor
- Asking friends who have been through the same situation or others (teachers, sibling, social worker, minister, etc.) for feedback on the problem
- Telling a trusted friend or adult that you need help and support
- Participating in a group activity (club, team, etc. that makes you feel good)
- Volunteering
- Participating in a support group (like this one!)

 Rewards and Recognition

- A special meal or treat
- A certificate of achievement
- Buying something special
- A celebration
- Scheduling time for an activity you enjoy
- A letter acknowledging what you've achieved (You can write it yourself or ask a close friend, teacher, or mentor to write one)

 Seeking Information

- Writing for yourself to find out what you think/feel
- Asking friends who have been through the same situation or others (teachers, sibling, social worker, minister, etc.) for feedback on the problem
- Reading books related to the issue
- Interviewing someone about the subject
- Viewing reliable, trusted Internet sites to find out more
- Talking to a therapist/counselor

 Reflection and Experimentation

- Thinking/writing about the good things that could come out of your change
- Thinking/writing about the situation from the perspective of someone else who is involved in the change
- Figuring out ways to replace some of what you are losing and then trying out those ways
- Trying to act differently than you normally would and finding out how that feels
- Using a creative activity to express and think about your feelings (painting, drawing, composing music or poetry, etc.)

Sample Transitions Journals

Introduction

The teens who participated in the first Transitions workshops kept journals, which they used to write about their progress. They did it partly so that we could see how the discussion and activities were working, and improve them. But they found that all that writing and reflection deepened their learning.

In addition to the weekly Closing Reflections, you may want to consider keeping a separate Transitions diary to reflect on what you're learning and how you are changing. Here are some samples from the journals of the teens in the first few workshops to show you the kinds of things they were thinking about, the challenges they were facing, and how they met them.

Taking Control of My Life

By P.

Lately I've been extremely depressed. On the surface, everything is going really well for me. I just got an after-school job and I was accepted to a good college, so I'm on my way to independence. But I've also been dealing with a lot of painful experiences and feelings.

My boyfriend and I have been talking about breaking up. We've been together for two years, so that would be a big loss. I've also been unhappy about my living situation. A year ago I moved from kinship care with my grandmother to a new foster home. I still haven't adjusted. Finally, my twin sister, who has been diagnosed with schizophrenia, has been in the hospital. She's gained tons of weight from her medicine, started smoking, and has been acting wild.

When I think about my sister I just feel like I've failed. For years I have been trying to reach out to her and understand her illness. I try hard to support my sister and be a good influence, but I feel like all the advice and support I give means nothing if she continues to not take her medication and to get into trouble in the streets all the time.

I've tried to pretend that I'm not affected by what's going on. But with all of these stressful situations in my life, I've felt hopeless and have been putting myself down for a long time now. I'm frustrated with myself because it seems that no matter how hard I try, I can never seem to keep myself in order. A majority of the time I feel horrible about myself, and on a daily basis my feelings of depression interfere with my performance at work and school. It also makes me feel bad that I have received very little support from family and friends. Even though I need to focus on my job and get ready for college, it's hard for me to feel confident and stay focused on my goals.

I joined the Transitions workshop to get some help with the practical and emotional challenges I'm facing. In the group, we were going to learn some "tools"—creative ways to work toward making changing in our lives. But when we started meeting as a group, I had a hard time admitting out loud that I had any problems. I had gotten so used to covering up the emotions that had crept up inside of me. Usually, I try to avoid feeling what I'm feeling in order to protect myself from having to bear any more pain.

But the other participants in the group challenged me, and I had to realize that I wasn't resolving my issues by putting them on the shelf. They helped me realize that it's OK to admit that I have been in a period of crisis. To get through the crisis, I decided to sit down and really think about what I want to be when I grow up, and what goals I plan to achieve.

First I decided to write down all my goals:

—I want to major in sociology in college and earn a master's degree in social work.

—I want to take the foster care system by storm and change the system for the better so that the next generation of youth in care won't go through the difficult circumstances I've faced.

—I want to be the next Maya Angelou and reach out in my writing especially to people of color. I want to improve my writing, and find my voice. I want to be able

APPENDIX

to clarify what message I'm trying to convey to my readers. I want to be proud and to honestly be able to say that I have done my part in this world.

I decided that my goal during the workshop would be to find new ways to make myself happy. Instead of panicking and feeling like a complete failure when something goes wrong, I want to remember that every cloud has a silver lining. A transition is a process that doesn't happen over night. I'll have to stay focused on my goals and opportunities, even at the times when I'm miserable and just want to feel sorry for myself.

WEEK 1

This week I was filled with excitement and determination to fulfill my first task—starting a new scrapbook. I kept a scrapbook while I was living with my grandmother, and it helped me feel more at peace and relaxed. I still keep it tucked safely in the top drawer of my dresser.

So far, re-starting my scrapbook-keeping has been lovely. I have already posted quotes from role models and writers that I adore like James Baldwin, Maya Angelou, Oprah Winfrey and F. Scott Fitzgerald.

The only negative this week was a risk I took to write a letter to my foster mom, just for myself. I wrote about my true feelings towards her. While writing this letter I was overwhelmed at the amount of anger I had built up inside of me. I realized that I wanted a lot more support from her than she'd been giving me. I felt overwhelmed by this realization because all along I've acted as if things were great between us. I was lying to myself. Mixed emotions of pain and relief stirred through my head, but I also felt good about admitting to myself that I felt wounded and that this home was not a good place for me.

WEEK 2

This week I decided to be organized and structured in my approach to the workshop. I plan to set specific goals for myself each week, and tell the group if I am meeting them. I will be keeping a chart to take note of my progress. I feel that the chart will give a tremendous boost to my confidence about aging out because I will prove to myself that I am accomplishing my goals.

At times I feel unsure about myself and the path I want to follow. I have all lot of insecurities about not being prepared enough to age out of care and I worry a lot about whether I'll be able to finish all the things I need to do. Worrying actually causes me to lose my focus on my goals. When things don't seem to go my way—like if I don't get a high grade in math class—I tend to doubt myself and remind myself of what a failure I am.

When I wrote down my goals for this week, I was able to accomplish most of them, like talking to my social worker about aging out and signing up for a secretarial course. When I looked at the chart I felt good about all I'd accomplished.

The week wasn't all blissful, though. I've been upset about work because I feel like

I'm being treated unfairly since I'm so young. A lot of times I'm being scolded by one of the assistant managers for minor mistakes. I get really upset when I'm yelled at. I've been trying my best to not get too discouraged and to think differently about my mistakes—I try to turn them into lessons to carry me through the work world.

To maintain my positive attitude and remained focused, I also jot down my thoughts in my scrapbook whenever I'm feeling overwhelmed by an issue at my job. I feel I am lifting a lot of weight off of my shoulders and I'm more relaxed once I express my thoughts on paper.

Today, I also decided to stop by a bargain store and treat myself to several bamboo plants and a vase to showcase in my room. I feel good about rewarding myself for once. I love plants and feel more relaxed when I have them around.

WEEK 3

I finally completed this week's list of goals. The biggest task was attending a work force program orientation. The work force program helps people get started in their careers, and I think I need the training because of the problems I've been running into at my job. I also know that to reach my goals, I need to rise above my minimum wage salary.

At the workforce program orientation, I felt awkward being the only adolescent huddled in a room crowded with mostly immigrant adults. It was three hours long and boring, but worth it. I left the orientation with confidence and high hopes.

My goal is to complete the program and earn a MOUS certificate, which proves that I know how to use Microsoft programs, type, and maintain a computer.

At the end of the week I felt good about checking off my list of completed tasks. I'm making progress! My future appears clearer to me than before. I feel more in control and more in charge of my life.

WEEK 4

This week, everyone in the group looked back at where we started and where we are now. Even though I'm making progress, I feel as if the tools I'm doing just aren't quite enough. For the last week I've been feeling depressed. I blame it on the workshop because even though I've been working so hard, I still feel awful. I still have to cope with my sister being in the hospital, the issues in my relationship, and the situation in my foster home, which is depressing.

After thinking for a while, I decided that focusing only on practical solutions wasn't going to help me feel better. In order to get new ideas of how to cope with my emotional life, I made the decision to seek information from friends and family. For once I was brave enough to admit that I was out of answers and desperately in need of help.

I browsed through my phone book and called several friends that I knew I could rely on. After an hour of pouring my heart out to one of my girlfriends, I felt more at ease. It felt good to put my sad feelings out in the open. After our conversation, I felt reassured that I had someone to turn to for advice and support. I decided to start working towards building a strong support system around me. I feel more secure knowing that I have people I can turn to when feeling down and out.

On Sunday I attended a Buddhist Temple with my aunt. My aunt has been practicing Buddhism for six years. I feel good vibes every time I go to the temple. The people there are very kind and together. After meetings, I'm spiritually relaxed and comfortable.

WEEK 5

From being in the group, I have also realized that I have a self-esteem issue. I want to do something that can me help find ways to improve how I think of myself. I decided to start reading books to help with the issues that I am facing in life. Reading puts me in another world and makes me feel cozy and relieved. But reading also makes me think a lot about my own personal life.

My book this week was "Caucasia," about a girl who is half-black and half-white. The story raised a lot of questions about race that I've had myself. Often I feel out of place because as a light-skinned black girl, I'm stuck between the color line. Reading this book, I felt extra-privileged to be an African-American woman, almost as if I was part of a secret organization that people outside my race could never come into or understand.

I enjoy reading books that boost my self-esteem and give me a better understanding of who I am. I feel more secure once I gain more knowledge about issues that are troubling me.

I am still keeping up my practical tasks, though. I started filling out an application online for ETVs, which helps foster youth pay for tuition and school expenses. And I called my caseworker to discuss more plans about aging out of foster care.

WEEK 6

My breakup with my boyfriend has continued to be a problem for me. I fear that I am losing too much of my focus on important things. I'm also running out of money because I have to run to the corner store for ice cream every time I get upset just thinking about him.

Finally I decided to give away my cell phone for several weeks to avoid having any contact with my boyfriend. That enabled me to find my own independence and to pay more attention to myself.

CONCLUSIONS

Looking back over the Transitions workshop, I think that keeping this diary has helped me discover a lot about myself. I realized that all my life I have been running from my fears. But trying to ignore problems, like the isolation I feel in my foster home and the helplessness I feel when I think about my sister's illness, doesn't make them go away. I realized that I feel better when I write talk to friends and family about how I am feeling, and when I take steps to deal with the practical issues I'm facing. Keeping the chart helped me feel that I can approach practical tasks with confidence. Beginning a new scrapbook, buying myself a few plants, going to the Buddhist temple with my aunt, and eating ice cream all made me feel a little better about the situations I can't control that are causing me pain. I feel more prepared to meet my future challenges now. I don't plan on falling into depression every time I feel as if I've reached a dead end.

I feel confident and proud of myself for completing the workshop, because it wasn't easy. I noticed that at times it was difficult for me to use the tools, because some tools were too risky. Writing the letter to my foster mother was especially painful, because it made me have to face a situation I tried to ignore.

I plan to keep using the Transition tools, especially writing my goals and thoughts in my scrapbook. My scrapbook documents all my ideas and aspirations. I feel good knowing that two years from now I will have my scrapbook to look at to remind me of who I was during this rocky time.

Gaining Trust in Friends

By M.

It's been over two years since I left my residential treatment center. I was no longer a resident, but I would visit the campus to see my friends. Things were good, but sometimes when I would visit things would feel weird, like I didn't know who my friends really were. We used to have common interests such as bagging girls, partying and playing basketball, but now there is not much we have in common. My friends are still bagging girls and going to parties, but it's no longer my thing. I am into settling down with my current girl and remaining close to home.

Many of my friends haven't grown up and are still living the lifestyle they did when they were on the campus. Living on the campus was easy living because everything was taken care of. They provided clothing money, food and transportation. The residents didn't have to pay bills, either. The only responsibilities were to go to school, do chores and stay in program.

I was able to work on campus, so whatever money I made I would buy video games, slam magazines and save money for a rainy day. My friends were allowed to work also. They would spend all their money on kicks and the latest fashions that dropped. Now that I'm on my own I still buy things I want, but not until all my bills are paid. But my friends spend every cent on unnecessary things no matter if their bills are paid or not—and then they turn to me for help.

I would like to help my friends out because that is what friendship is all about, but I am unsure if I should trust everyone because I am worried they will use me. I want friends I won't have to question myself about, friends that are level headed and staying out of trouble. My goal for the Transitions workshop is to rebuild my trust in friends. I hope that by using the tools I can find ways to help separate the friends I feel close to from the ones I am unsure about.

WEEK 1

I chose rituals and ceremonies for my tool. I made it a ritual to call my friends at least once a week to keep me from feeling distant from them. I felt good about my decision because it would help me stay in contact with friends despite my feelings about being unsure on whether or not I could trust everyone. I feel keeping in contact with friends and observing the conversations we have will help me with my trust issues.

This week I called a friend up on the phone to see what was good on his side of town. The conversation was filled with laughter. We joked about a party over the weekend when friends of an old friend of mine were fighting over a girl from the group home.

Overall: A

WEEK 2

Last week went well and I hoped that this week would be the same, but things didn't turn out as planned. I invited a friend to chill with me since I decided to surround myself with things that remind me of good times or make me feel comfortable and peaceful. We played video games and talked about old times. I thought being around an old friend would give me a sense of peace, but instead I felt down. I loved remembering the good times, but I felt a little depressed about it too, because those times are in the past and I have to be focused on the present.

I tried to talk to my friend about how he's doing now, but he didn't say much. Since he didn't want to get into detail I decided not to continue the conversation. The sudden silence when I would bring up the present gave me a feeling he wasn't doing too well. I didn't want to brag about how well things were going for me, knowing that things were going bad for him, and I didn't think it would do us any good to meddle into the past.

Overall: C+

WEEK 3

I chose to identify who could be helpful to me and who couldn't. I decided to create a social circle to figure out which of my friends support me the most. Then I could try to become closer with them, and distance myself from the ones who support me the least. My name is in the middle and my friends' names go around mine with lines connecting to my name. There are four types of lines. The double line represent "excellent" which means helping one another, being able to speak about anything and trust each other with deep things. The single line represent "good" which means that help is given sometimes, conversations are leveled and trust isn't an issue. The uneven line represents "fair," which means that help is undecided, conversations are basic and trust is sometimes a issue. The single line with an x in the middle represents "unhealthy," which means the friend is an associate and trust is an issue.

From doing the social circle I learned I don't have much support from my friends. They could come to me whenever they need help, but they don't return the help. Whenever I am in a jam I find ways to get myself out without asking for help, but it would be nice to know if I did ever need to ask my friends for a helping hand they'd be down.

Overall: B+

WEEK 4

I chose acting differently than I normally would and finding how it feels for my tool. A few of my friends called to ask for advice and I gave them my honest opinion, only for them to do the opposite. Why? I feel it's stupid for a person to ask someone for help if they have the intentions to do the complete opposite. Normally I wouldn't show them I was angry. When I feel bothered or annoyed by almost anything (petty or serious), I try not to get angry because I don't think straight and I might do something that I'll regret later. But since my tool was to act differently I wanted to see how it felt to release my anger. I expressed my anger with a high tone of voice and started telling them how they should make their own decisions and not ask me for advice if they are going to disregard it. I felt bad about screaming at them, but I also felt good to let out some anger (but not too much).

Overall: B-

WEEK 5

I didn't have a legit tool because I couldn't think of one that related to my transition goal. My editor wrote some questions for me to answer about how I worry so much and how it relates to my goal about not being able to trust certain friends. I answered the questions the best way I could. I learned that I worry so much because I didn't have healthy boundaries with my friends. I didn't think I needed any until one of my friends called on Wednesday to asked to stay over because he was in a tight situations and I told him he could stay 'til Friday.

APPENDIX

When he came to the house he had his girl with him. He never mentioned anything to me about her tagging along, but I didn't mind at the time because I thought both our girls could get to know each other. I felt it would be a good idea for him to stay a few days for me to work on my trust issues.

I wanted to make everyone including myself feel comfortable by watching movies, talking, and playing video games together. But things didn't turn out as planned. My friend and his girl stayed to themselves cuddled up on the pull-out bed like they were in a hotel. Things began to get out of hand when Friday came and he asked to stay until Sunday. I was cool, but when Monday came and he was still around I started to get angry. He and his girl started to get too comfortable. I don't think he was in a tight situation, but just wanted to spend some alone time with his girl. I didn't like how he made me believe that he was in trouble. If he wanted to bring his girl and stay over to be together then I have no problem with it, but he didn't have to lie. I told him they had to leave, and that I would have to think about whether or not I would let him stay overnight in the future. I don't feel bad about telling him to leave because I see it as my first step in setting boundaries.

Overall: A+

WEEK 6

My last but not least tool is to ask myself, "Now that the old way has ended, what are my options?" My options are limited, but I've decided to have standard boundaries with my friends to protect myself from being used, worried and angry. I want them to set boundaries with me, too. I'd like to come to a mutual understanding about crossing boundaries with at least three friends.

I want to tell my friends why I've been acting differently around them. I don't know if they would take it the wrong way, but they need to know that things have changed. I like the idea of discussing this with my friends because they'll know that I'm not the same guy I was a couple years back, but a different, more mature person. Then I can see if they accept me this way or not. Maybe they can take what I'm telling them to help them to grow from the things they couldn't let go of. I can't be the one to get them out of trouble all the time, they need to learn how to get themselves out of trouble or prevent it from happening. I have a responsibility to look after myself, and they have to understand that. I'm going to be distant from the friends who won't accept my boundaries, because I know they are the kind of people I don't want around me.

Flipping the Script
How I stopped putting myself down.

By H.

(You read some of this journal in Session 3. This is the complete journal.)

"Listen to the beat," says Melissa, wincing at the sight of my dancing. "Now lean wit' it."

"Damn, how I'm black and I ain't got no rhythm? Ain't that supposed to be a given?"

"Sometimes I wonder about you…" Melissa says, sarcastically. "Let's keep it simple to just the snap." I try to snap and end up like a white person putting up the crip sign (it just won't work).

I zone out in thought: "Why am I so slow? Lord Jesus, why don't I get it? How stupid can one person be? It's just a snap. Then again, Lord Jesus can't help my dumb ass even with the Twelve Apostles. Why try? Is it really going to help? I can be quite the retard."

That's the type of thing I think at least three times a day—until I take a deep breath in and repeat the following words: "OK, I'm not that slow." Then I exhale all the negative energy.

Expecting the Worst

Whenever I try something new I feel very discouraged. I always think things are going to go wrong, maybe because in the past many things have. For instance, I liked my group home and was comfortable there. Did I think that was going to last? No! And it didn't. I was shipped off to a foster home. People predicted it would be good and I said it would be bad. Guess who was right? I was.

After years of disappointments, I don't have confidence that almost anything will have a positive outcome. I predict things will go wrong so that when they do, I'm not surprised. It's a way of getting used to the many shortcomings in my life and of protecting myself from getting let down.

I also constantly tell myself that I'm dumb so that insults from others don't hurt too bad. That started when teachers, kids at school and even my family teased me and called me names. Repeating those taunts to myself lessened the pain I felt when I heard them from others.

Holding Myself Back

Although these are good strategies for handling disappointments, I recently realized that they're also holding me back from fully enjoying my life. I don't get excited about new experiences because I fear they'll go wrong. And I don't feel as much pride and joy about what I do well because I'm bracing myself for the good times to go bad.

These days, my life is a lot more stable than it once was. I'm living in a better foster home, coming up on high school graduation and already accepted to a good college—SUNY Binghamton in upstate New York. I don't need to brace myself for failure anymore.

I need to work on my pessimistic attitude so I don't prevent myself from growing and living my life to the fullest. I hope to act more positive, enjoy things and attract positive people to me. I want to learn to accept the compliments people give me without using skepticism or sarcasm to downplay what they've said. And I want to stop beating myself up.

Flipping the Script

So this winter I joined the Transitions Workshop, a group where we learned new coping mechanisms (we called them "tools") to help us get through difficult changes. I chose to work on changing the negative script in my head. Here is the diary of my attempts to change how I think about myself:

March 16

This week I decided to keep tabs on myself and write down how often I criticize myself and what I say. Surprisingly, I found out I don't criticize myself as often as I thought, but when I do I'm really harsh. It's like, why do I need enemies when I've got myself? It shouldn't be that way.

As a way to motivate myself to eliminate the problem I decided to write down a reminder of why I need to make this change. I realized I've never been on a roller coaster or ridden a bike, and I can't swim or snap my fingers—all because I've never really tried. It was painful to face how I am holding myself back.

If I complete this change I may learn

how to do all those things, maybe even whistle. Those are little things, but they're steps toward my overall goal of building more confidence in myself and my abilities. My writing was a wake-up call that my constant self-criticism is not only crippling my self-esteem but also damaging my ability to try new things.

March 23

This week I wrote some more about my problem—this time putting down some of the terrible criticisms I heard as a child, like: "Why you sitting here talking to the quiet b-tch?" "I can't even sit next to her. Yo, shorty a straight weirdo."

I was shocked to remember that a girl in my class had the audacity to talk about me to my face. But writing down those insults surprised me because my feelings were less intense than I thought they would be, which was good. I even reread what I wrote, which I never do.

My journal writing left me in such good spirits that I decided on the first action I would take to change. I decided that for the rest of the week I'd tell myself good things anytime something negative happened.

Trying this technique also surprised me because it somewhat worked. If I started to criticize myself, I was able to stop and tell myself good things.

The problem was I didn't believe a word that was coming out of my mouth. I truly felt like a compulsive liar, and a bad one at that. Despite telling myself all these good things, I still felt incompetent deep down. But I think that I need to program my first thought to be positive, and eventually my feelings about myself might catch up.

April 6

Continuing with my theme of telling myself positive things, I planned this week to put Post-Its on my mirror with my positive characteristics written on each. That way each morning I'll wake up with good feelings about myself, and I'll be able to study my positive qualities. I also wrote an on-the-go list of my positive qualities in my journal so I'd always have it with me.

The list included: introspective, intelligent, considerate, understanding, timid, intuitive, intricate, broad-minded, caring, and able to disregard my emotions during times of stress.

I decided that I'd take a quiz about what's good about me. I know that may sound weird, but the best way to get an idea fixated into my brain is to study. I studied the list as if for a real test, and I kept repeating it to myself randomly. Sporadically during the day I would think, "I'm beautiful and an intellectual."

This plan was good because it helped me look in the mirror (which I hardly ever do). I'm definitely going to make this a routine.

Despite my list, I had a hard time when we discussed "self-esteem" in health class. It brought me back to my lowest moments of childhood; I kept remembering unpleasant memories that made me feel bad about myself. At least saying positive things about myself helped get my mind off those past memories.

April 13

This week I chose to write a story about a time in my life when I used all the positive characteristics I posted on my mirror. The story was a way to remind myself of my strength.

Here's what I wrote:

"When I was at home with my mom, she refused to talk to me. In fact, she refused to talk to any of her family. (She has schizophrenia and was addicted to crack for years.) Everyone else left her alone and ignored her crying.

"Although I was only 12, I was intelligent and intuitive enough to realize that my mom wasn't OK and needed help expressing herself. So instead of going to school, I was considerate and sensitive of her feelings—I stayed at home with her every day.

"I wasn't sad to miss school. When I was

younger, going to school was painful because I only had two outfits, my skin looked horrible, and my mom would mess up my hair. So you can imagine how much I got teased. (I am amazed that I go to school today.)

"That year I stayed home I was patient. I knew of my mom's violent nature, so I waited and eventually she opened up to me. She told me how she felt watched, and she pulled the blinds down. She told me that a boyfriend she had when she was 10 hypnotized her and was now having her watched. She claimed my father was in on it, telling 'Casper' of her whereabouts.

"As far-fetched as the story was, I listened and did not interrupt. The story was unreal, but her pain was not. The situation made me feel strong yet scared. It was good that my mom had me to turn to, but who did I have?

"Soon after that I was placed in foster care. I am involved with my family but remain detached emotionally so I am able to live and not let their needs consume me. I still visit them, to show them my loyalty and let them know that they are irreplaceable."

Writing all of this down, I reminded myself of my strength and resilience. It was good to remember that there are reasons I have trouble feeling positive about my life, but also that the worst times are behind me.

April 20

This week I meant to "seek social support"—surround myself with friends—because one thing I don't think I do well is communicate with new people. Because of the criticism I've experienced, and the way I criticize myself, I usually believe that others won't like me.

I meant to hold a sleepover, but that didn't work out, so instead I went on a college tour with another group member, Natasha. It went very well. I talked to kids on the bus, and Tasha and I talked to some college kids all by ourselves. We then finished the day off by going to my house and just chilling. I found out that I can communicate when I want to, if I'm around someone I like.

I also read a book called *The Joy of Doing Things Badly*, by Veronica Chambers. The book helped me realize that I should focus on making myself happy, because I owe myself more of my attention than I owe anybody else.

Veronica wrote about doing what you enjoy, even if you do it by yourself, and explained that you'll feel more confident if you surround yourself with what makes you feel good. Her book was a reminder to me that I'm not going to do everything well, and I don't need to criticize myself just because it takes time to learn new things.

Conclusions

While participating in this workshop, and writing this story, I've uncovered some interesting things about myself. I've realized that I'm stronger than I thought I was. I feel inspired to work on other aspects of my life that bother me. Maybe it is possible for me to be happier day to day.

Sometimes the group was stressful. I learned that I could participate in an intense group without freezing up or isolating myself. I bonded with the other writers and, for the first time, I had a strong social circle. That's helped me realize that people aren't going to criticize me if I let them in. I can communicate with people, and I can try to deal with my worst struggles.

Throughout the weeks of this workshop, I thought negatively about my planned tools and then found out they were effective at making me feel better. As it turns out, there are alternative ways I can approach the problems I am facing, rather than simply writing about them.

Even after the workshop is over, I plan to continue to write letters to myself because they help me express my inner anger, and to put words on my mirror, which helps me recognize my inner beauty. I've realized that being pessimistic takes joy from my life, and trying to be more positive has been a change worth making.

Getting Back My Joy
I'm trying to trade my bad memories for good ones.

By E.

All my happy memories were wiped away when I was very young, since I was in and out of foster care from the age of 2. I remembered things, but only negative things. I could remember the abuse and abandonment, but not the good times our family had.

Maybe it was because when I was in bad situations it was too painful for me to remember the good times. The happiness and joyful moments faded away and were replaced with fear and sadness.

Over time, I developed barriers like anger and hate that are still holding me back from healing. I tend to keep myself miserable and dissatisfied by dwelling on painful events in my life.

Last spring, I joined the Transitions workshop, where we could work on a change we wanted to make in our lives. I joined the workshop because I wanted to be more happy and less sad. I felt it was time to restore the happy memories I'd lost. I wanted to be able to listen to slow songs without crying, write poetry to express myself and read books related to my issues without it being too emotional for me to handle.

The workshop met once a week and at the beginning we wrote down our goals. My goal was to create a healing process for myself and start to collect new memories, so I

APPENDIX

wouldn't always be thinking about the negative memories from my painful past.

I would keep a detailed scrapbook that would be a written record of the change I started creating in my life. The book would be a memento I could look at to help me cope with pain.

Each week, we were supposed to try a different "tool" for handling change, and write about our progress. Here's the diary I kept, describing how my change went.

Week 1

I decided to start by interviewing someone—my mom.

On Friday March 24, my mother and I sat down and tried to figure out ways to remember good times we used to have. I said a little about the things I remembered and she filled in the missing pieces. My mother wasn't sure she could remember much and I wasn't either, but when we were done we had about six pages of good times we used to have. It was all coming back to me.

I remembered that around Christmas time we would go to Macy's department store to see Santa and to Toys "R" Us to shop for gifts. We bought a lot of things like board games and dolls. When we left it seemed as if we'd bought the whole store.

My mother also remembered how around Halloween time we would go shopping for costumes and makeup at a party store. We would go trick or treating at noon around the 'hood, to the pet shop and local candy stores. The pet shop would give out free goldfish. We would change makeup to hit the same places twice.

I remembered the whole family getting along and cooking for Thanksgiving. We had a feast and gave our six cats their own portion.

I loved the first day of school because I got to go shopping for school supplies and new clothes. According to my mom, I started school early and I was a bright child. I would line the kids up for bathroom time at Head Start. I would put the girls in one line and the boys in the other. I knew my ABC's and how to count to 20.

Even though my visit with my mom went well, I felt sad when I talked about it in the workshop. That seemed like a terrible setback, and I got stuck feeling like I couldn't handle the positive memories at all. I felt bad and low.

But after I went home to think things over, I had a breakthrough. I realized that seeing my mom was still difficult. What was really going on was that I missed my mom and felt abandoned all over again, even though I wasn't really being abandoned. I was struggling and having a low week. Then I got my bearings again.

Week 2

This week I decided to use the tool that asks you to think about what the change means to you, and what new opportunities it gives you. I thought about how creating this change is something I need to do for myself. No one else can create this change besides me, but others can be supportive and help me when help is needed.

It's up to me to do what needs to be done. I will be the one who benefits from a successful transition. I have an opportunity to change my way of thinking and restore my positive memories. I am determined to work toward whatever it is that will help me to feel better and enjoy my life more.

Week 3

This week I read a book called *How to Collect Happiness*. It tells you to make a "happiness list" every day, where you write down five things that happened that day that you feel good about. "These don't have to be Big Things," it says. "Think about the small things you usually don't notice that put a smile on your face."

Trying to heal from my broken past is taking a lot out of me. It's a good deed I am doing, but it's hard because for so long I have been wearing a mask and I don't know what it looks like under the mask. Am I capable of recovering the joy I once had and collecting happiness? Or did I completely lose the person that once felt happy?

When I started writing down good things that happened each day, it really did help me feel happier and less depressed. I think the book helps more than my mood stabilizers.

By reading the book I learned a little bit about how to collect happiness, but not how to keep it.

Week 4

Recently I realized that I have to get rid of my first TV, and I fear that I will lose the memories behind it. I bought the TV at a yard sale one hot summer when my caseworker and I went shopping. It is special for me because it's the first TV I owned. It leaves a memory of my old group home and staff.

I don't want to throw the TV away, but it's taking up space. For me to get new furniture and make myself feel better in a clean and well organized home, I have to make sacrifices, even if that means throwing away some important things I have grown to love.

I will take a picture of the TV and place it in my scrapbook, so that I can always look at the picture and remember the good memories. I may not have the TV in my home, but I will still have the memories stored inside the picture. Whenever I miss my TV I can pull out the picture and reminisce. When I finish coping with my loss I will treat myself to a private junk food party.

Week 5

This week I have taken pictures of things I like such as a gift that was given to me, places I like to go and things at home that keep me motivated. I also decided to put pictures of family, friends, my cat and myself up on my wall to help me remember good times.

Now when I go to bed, I look up at my photo wall. The pictures always make me happy, because they remind me of good times I've had. It helps me sleep peacefully. I am going to take a picture of the wall and place it inside my scrapbook, so I can see it even when I'm not at home. I hope remembering happy times will help me collect happiness.

Week 6

I had the giggles earlier today. I felt good! It's about time I give in to laughter and remember what made me happy as a child, and then go out and get some of that same innocent joy back in my life.

Conclusions

When I first began the Transitions workshop I thought I was beginning the new chapter of my new identity. But after a few weeks passed I realized I was nowhere close to ready for a new start. I was in Letting Go, the first stage of a transition, on saying goodbye to my negative thoughts and bad memories. And I was only a little further along on remembering happy memories.

I now understand that I have not reached a point where I totally feel comfortable with myself. I have worked hard to forget about negative things, yet I feel like by letting go of the negative things I am taking a piece of myself away.

I want people to know and understand that this is who I am and I have worked hard to get to this point. But the problem is that now that I am at this point I am scared. In life there are good things, but bad things always seem to follow. It's like I am battling myself for happiness.

Still, by starting to create a change in the Transitions workshop, I feel empowered to care for myself and seek help and support when needed.

I really want to keep using these tools as a big part of healing and moving on to bigger, better things in the future. Every time I take a positive step towards making change in my life, I will reward myself. And now I have some new happy memories to look back on with a smile.

Alternate Lesson for Letting Go (Session 5)

Following is another activity to learn about the Letting Go stage. It involves reading one of the following three stories, which were all written by teens who were struggling with loss, and thinking about the questions on this worksheet with a partner or in a small group. You may or may not use this lesson in your workshop. If you don't, feel free to read the stories on your own—they can help you reflect on the difficulties of letting go, and how to find ways to move forward.

Learning How to Let Go

After your team takes turns reading aloud the assigned story, discuss and answer together the following questions.

Story title: _____

Author: _____

1. Describe the transition that the writer is going through: What was the big change s/he went through, and what is the change s/he is trying to make?

2. What is the writer losing (good or bad) in this transition?

3. What is hard for the writer about letting go? What prevents him/her from letting go, and how does being stuck in the Letting Go stage affect him/her?

4. Thinking about your toolkit, what tools do you think would be most helpful to the writer in finding his/her way through the Letting Go stage? Why?

Letting It Out
I can't hide anymore from the grief inside me.

Cynthia Orbes

By Cynthia Orbes

When I was very young I thought my future would be typical—I would finish high school and go to college with my mom helping me along, and my mom would be there when I got married. I never could have imagined that by the time I was 10 years old both my parents would have died and my sister and I would be living with people we didn't know.

A Safe Place

The neighborhood my family lived in when I was small was calm and clean. We had a safe playground with trees here and there. I remember my father pushing me on the swings.

My family's apartment was the greatest. We had a big kitchen and a cellar and a backyard with a tree. My sister and I used to ride our bikes and play in the mud.

My mother couldn't do much because as far back as

I can remember she was in a wheelchair. But she liked to read to me. My father was sometimes kind to me too, like when he took me to school or called me "sweetness," or when he let me help him cook.

But by the time I turned 6 I knew something was wrong. My mom and dad yelled at each other a lot. My mother would cry and sometimes my father stormed out of the apartment cursing. I hated it when my mother cried. I would run to her and hug her. I worried that my dad would hurt my mom.

My parents also drank all the time. It made me feel bad to be around them when they were drinking. It was like watching my mother and father fall apart. I could tell they were not too happy and I felt sorry for them.

Then my father got sick with cancer and was in the hospital. I missed him and I wanted to see him but my mother would never take me. He died right before my 8th birthday. I couldn't tell him goodbye.

Even my father's death did not make my mother stop drinking. And we had to move a month later because the landlord doubled our rent.

Too Many Changes

When my mother told me that we were moving, I was so mad. Too many things were changing. I did not want to leave the house that I grew up in and move to some old junk place. I did not want to leave all my friends. I did not want to go to a new school. I liked my life the way it was.

The new apartment that we moved to was small, and my mother told us that it was not a very good neighborhood. We could tell because the buildings looked so run down and old and there were many projects. It was dangerous on the north side and down by the pier.

I'd complain and say, "I want to leave, I hate it here." My mother told me that we would not stay for long, just until we found a better place. I believed her until a couple of months passed and I realized that we were going to stay there. So I dropped it. I just had to become used to this new life.

But after two years my mother passed away, too. I was filled with sorrow and disbelief. I wanted everything to go back to the way that it was. I wanted to rewind time.

For years afterward, I was angry. I felt abandoned. I could not believe that I had to go on the rest of my years without parents. I even stopped believing in God, because I couldn't believe there could be a reason for what happened to me.

Stranded in Foster Care

The day my mother died, the cops came and took my sister and me to an office to wait for a foster home. I was thinking, "Where am I going? Who is going to take care of me?"

We got into a foster home that night. It was a big, beautiful house, but I felt stranded. I only felt protected around my sister and followed her everywhere she went. She didn't like that I'd become an annoying shadow that crept behind her.

After I got into foster care, I had a lot of people telling me not to be sad. They said, "You cannot change the past so you are just going to have to deal with it." So I tried not to think about my feelings.

When people asked me if I was OK, I would say that I was, although behind my smiles were held-back tears. Eventually people stopped asking.

On the anniversary of my mother's death, my 6th grade teacher told me, "Cynthia, you're going to have a lot more days like this to come. You just have to be strong about it." Her words made me feel strong enough to handle my life, but it did not help the pain go away.

Creating My Fantasy Life

I tried so hard to forget what happened and pretend that my mother was somewhere watching over me. I started reading fantasy books that kept my mind off my mother's death and let me live in a fake world.

If I spent too much time in the foster home I'd end up thinking, "Why am I here? Is it real?" I'd remember when my mother would get her check and would take us out to eat at McDonald's, our favorite place. Or when my mom would cook. I just liked knowing she was in the kitchen cooking. My favorite was chicken cutlet.

Thinking about the nice times would make me sad and then I'd get mad because I didn't want to be sad. So I would try to ignore my memories and pretend that my past wasn't real. It made me feel a little better to tell myself, "I've always lived with Miss Molly. My life started at 10."

Once Miss Molly told me, "Whenever you're ready, put a picture of your mom on your dresser to remind you of her." I thought, "I'm not doing that. Are you crazy?" I thought it would make me too sad to look at her. It would be like being at her funeral again.

Angry and Scared

I hated life. I was afraid to care about anything or anyone because I thought I would lose them. That feeling of loss—I was tired of that feeling. I did not want to lose any more things that I liked, loved or had become used to.

I was so afraid that I became really stubborn. I remember my sister yelling at me once about something important. I said, "I don't care!"

"Well, you better start caring," she said. I paused, and then I said, "I don't care," in a calm, sure voice.

To keep from thinking about the past, I tried to stay busy. I spent all my free time reading or with friends, my sister, my mentor, and, as I got older, my boyfriend.

Alone in the House

Then, a couple years ago, I got in trouble with my foster mother. I had to stay in the house after school for several months. I felt very alone in the house. I needed to feel close to my friends and act crazy to let out my feelings.

In school, memories of my past began to distract me. I'd look at the window knowing I would not be able to go outside after school. That made me think about my parents and my problems more. I felt overwhelmed and suffocated but did not want to break down.

I only cried once.

After I stopped crying I realized I couldn't be in my foster home anymore. My sadness would lead me to other terrible memories, like my mom's funeral and the times my father would drink a lot.

I began to leave school early so I'd have enough time to get to the park and play handball before going home.

Even though I didn't want to cut school, I needed to. Handball relieved some of my stress and made me feel a little better.

My Past Is Getting Stronger

I hoped that I could just keep on distracting myself from the pain of my past. But in the last few years, my past has been stronger in my mind and my "I don't care" attitude changed to "Please help me. I am alone right now and desperately need some guidance."

That feeling that I am alone is always with me. My foster mom doesn't really take care of me, and even though I have my sister and she cares a crazy amount about me, she doesn't live with me anymore and is not my caretaker.

Sometimes the feeling of being abandoned and scared is so strong. Sometimes when I have a lot of homework and responsibilities, I have a hard time being positive. I start saying to myself, "I can't do this on my own with all of this pressure." I want help from my parents at those times.

Thinking About My Parents

Once in school we watched a movie about the health effects of smoking. It showed people who were dying from it. I began thinking about my mother, saying to myself, "People waste their lives because they don't think about the side effects until it's too late."

I left school and went to the store, almost in tears. I wished my parents could've found another way besides drinking and smoking to keep themselves from feeling so sad. It's easier said than done, but I feel angry that they let their sadness ruin their lives and ours.

Just a few weeks ago, I broke down.

It happened on a Monday night. When I got to my foster home I wanted to be alone to try to figure out why I was feeling so bad and depressed. So I walked in to the bathroom and locked the door.

I thought how my life would have been with my parents. I thought about how bad my life is without them and I felt forsaken.

That Sad Part Underneath

The scary and upsetting part is that I think of myself as being strong emotionally. That's always been my biggest characteristic. It's very important to me to seem and act strong. I fear that, like my parents, I might get sadder and sadder and never feel better.

When I look back at my parents, I wish they had done some more positive things to help themselves with their sadness, instead of escaping by smoking and drinking. At least I use positive ways to take care of myself, like keeping busy, listening to music, reminding myself of my goals in life and spending time with my sister. Being able to stay strong makes me believe I can get through life.

I fear that if I let my feelings out everyone is going to see me as this sad and depressed girl and I don't want to be that girl. But now I think I have to open up that sad part underneath, because I have feelings from my past that I really need to deal with. I feel like my brain is telling me that I can't continue to hide.

Starting Over Without Them
I had to get out from under my mother's addiction

By H.

When I was 13, I stopped going to school. The kids called me retarded and I had no friends. All I thought about was going home to play cards and watch TV with my mom. Being at home comforting my mom was a way to get away from the torment of school and to play my role in the family—daughter and psychiatrist to my mom.

Not the Way a Kid Should Live

I was 9 when my dad told me that he and my mom were schizophrenic. He was scared of people but could function. He was able to work. He said my mother had it worse. She heard voices and thought people were trying to drive her crazy and to kill her. To cope with the pain, she started smoking crack.

Soon her addiction started to show. She would steal

money from the family. Sometimes we'd have no food in the house and would have to go to churches or beg at the welfare office. It made me feel embarrassed. I'd think, "This is not the way a kid should live, begging for food." I felt like she didn't care about me, because if she did, why would she spend our food money on crack?

Most of the time she was high and fidgety. When I touched her, she'd jump. Other times my mother would cry because of the voices and my dad would argue with her over her drug habit.

"You going to smoke up all the money," Dad would say.

"Please, just one more smoke," Mom would say.

My brother and I used to think, "Dad, why are you letting her do this to us?"

When I stopped going to school, a typical day with my mom started with her using half of the food money on crack and then coming home and smoking it. I'd usually check on her (because I could hear her talking to the voices) and she'd tell me to tell the voices to stop hurting her. I'd say a prayer for her and we'd play her favorite card game or watch television while I held her.

Then I'd give her my usual lecture, telling her the voices are only in her head. I'd make clear that I didn't want to hurt her. I'd tell her she has a mental illness. My mom would hold me and cry when I comforted her.

Angry and Abandoned

I was afraid to leave her alone. It was hard feeling responsible for her, and sometimes it was overwhelming because I had my own problems. I also felt it wasn't a child's place to take care of her mother.

It was especially confusing to know that my mom was not in control of the way she acted. I'd tell myself not to be upset, because she wasn't trying to hurt me. But as much as I tried to understand, I also felt angry and abandoned. Even now I don't think I can ever forgive my mom for spending the food money. I think to myself, "If you really loved me, why would you do that to me? You saw how I was suffering."

Avoiding the World

Over time I got depressed. When I woke in the morning, I didn't want to leave the house because I felt like the world had nothing to offer me. At home I would cry. My frustration made me start eating a lot. I used to weigh more than 185 pounds.

My mother doing drugs had me feeling like life wasn't worth living. Eventually I figured I should just stay at home and avoid the world.

When I stopped going to school, I didn't think anybody would realize I was gone, but the attendance office called ACS, the child welfare agency in New York City.

All Alone in Care

When I entered foster care, I was terrified. The first week, I stayed in my room and cried day and night. It was strange not to wake up and watch TV or play video games, and to have nobody to say "I love you" to. I just wanted to go back home.

Being in care felt scary because I knew my mom had nobody to console her. My parents came to visit every weekend. I felt better then because we'd go out for a walk and my mom would cry on my shoulder just like the old days.

But I soon began to feel relieved that the weight of my family's problems had been lifted off my shoulders. I realized that caring for my mom was hurting my life, and that she needs more help than a child can give.

Focused on Myself

As I got settled into my group home, I realized I hadn't been getting all of the attention I needed at home and it felt good to focus on myself. There was not a lot of stress in the group home and if I needed someone to talk to there was always a staff on duty. I felt good knowing I had staff that led me in the right way and girls that helped lift my spirits. That's when I started to think that foster care is where I need to be.

In the group home, I can focus on my education and try to deal with my fear of people before it gets worse. I've started interacting with the girls and opening up about the anger I felt toward my mom by telling a new friend what I'd been going through at home.

During the first year of living without my parents, my depression lifted tremendously. As I talked more about my feelings and let them out, I didn't wake up crying like I did at home and I lost the weight I'd gained.

I started to realize that the world has many wonderful things to offer me, because I started to go outside, hang out with my friends and have fun. I was even able to go back to school and keep up an 85 average.

The Option to Leave

I realized that my depression was caused by stress at home and my failure to be able to communicate with people at school and make friends. Now I know that the only worries I need to have are about me, myself and I. It feels great to feel stronger and in control.

On my home visits, I saw nothing had changed. I felt glad that I could go see my family, but I also appreciated being able to leave when things got too intense. I wanted to be close to my mom, to let her know I care for her and that she's not alone in this world, but I also felt like I needed to stay detached so her problems won't affect me the way they used to. Now when her problems become unbearable, it's back to my home away from home.

Releasing My Anger

Not being surrounded by them has also me realize how mad I feel. I've always tried to cover up my feelings when I'm with my mom, because I figured that she has enough stress without knowing that she hurts me. But lately my feelings have been hurt so bad I can't cover them up, like when I think about how my mom and dad let us starve.

Then I blow up, screaming and yelling, "Shut the f-ck up and leave me the f-ck alone!" My mom will say, "MoMo (that's my nickname), what did I do to upset you? Why do you act like this? I love you." Instead of telling her what's wrong I'll hold her and say, "Sorry, I love you."

I only outburst once in a while but it makes me feel calm and refreshed to let my feelings out and to stand up to my mom and give her what she deserves. It's frightening, too, because sometimes I feel like I might never stop.

Since I came into foster care, I've realized how much it affects me to hold so much in. Sometimes I feel confused because I wonder, "Is it OK to feel sympathetic and angry at the same time? And if I always release the sympathetic side, where is all my anger going? And if I don't want to hurt my mother, when or how will I release my rage?"

Any blind man can see that my parents want me home, because they ask me, "When are you coming home?" and take me to my bedroom and ask me to spend a night. But can they actually care for me? I think not. So after being in care for a year, I decided that going home would be a setback.

'I Don't Want to Go Home'

In July, at my Service Plan Review, my social worker told my mom that I don't want to go home and my mom asked, "Is that true?" I said, "Yes." She asked, "Why, MoMo? We love you." Before she could start acting like a baby, my social worker cut her off. That day, my social worker also had my mom take a drug test. Of course she tested positive, so my social worker might try to convince her to get help.

When I left I felt good. I need to let her know I'm angry at her and that everything between us isn't peaches and cream. I feel like I'm being selfish, but I have to help myself.

I do have doubts about putting myself first, though. I wonder, "Who is my mom going to have?" And it's scary to focus on myself. Before, whenever I was confused or frustrated about my own problems, I could focus on my mom instead. Now I have nobody else's problems to get me away from my reality.

My Parents Don't Understand

I don't think my parents really understand my decision to stay in foster care. And I think my mom is confused when I say that she's mistreated me, because she really can't seem to see what she did wrong.

For so long I never showed the way I feel about her, so I think my mom still does not understand that her drug habit affects me. Maybe the only way she'll understand is if I tell her straight up or call the police on her when she smokes or buys crack.

Right now, I think it's better for me to wonder what she knows than to know for sure, because I don't want to find out the answer. Maybe I'll have the courage to find out someday.

Taking Myself to Anger School
It's not helping me to feel rage at the world.

Eric Green

By Eric Green

This fall I decided to make handling my anger my project because I'd gotten into expressing it too freely. I've been through a lot of negative things in my life. As I grew up, anger became the only feeling left in me.

It's hard for me to communicate calmly with people because of the anger inside of me. I often respond with anger because I don't know another way. This makes my relationships with friends and family difficult.

Hard Times at Home

My anger brings me back to the time before I entered foster care, when I felt frustrated and powerless because my biological parents neglected my brothers and me. They were smoking and drinking, and because of their habits, there was nothing in the house. No food to eat and no beds to sleep in. I remember sleeping with my brother William and our father on a mattress with no sheets.

My older brothers had to go outside and look for food. William once brought home a few half-eaten cheeseburgers. As we were eating them, I suddenly realized that I hadn't seen my mother and father in days. I asked, "Where's Mom? Where's Daddy?" William and I cried because they weren't home with us.

Feeling Like a Victim

Another part of my anger stems from my first foster home. Living there, I felt neglected and uncared for. The foster mother liked me but said I was a troublemaker and a bad influence.

Her son James was a bully from head to toe. Whenever I got in trouble he would stick his tongue out at me. I would get so upset. Out of pure frustration I once took a knife and planned to stab him. My brother William took a metal bat and planned to whack him. Luckily, we realized we were overreacting.

I also got teased a lot in school, even during kindergarten. When kids bullied me I felt I had no choice but to use my anger to protect myself. I remember biting one kid's finger and dumping my lunch tray on another kid's head.

Then there was the day when I was coming out of school and two kids suddenly started beating me up. I tried to break myself free from the fight but I couldn't. Those times made me feel like a victim, and now when I feel powerless, I get angry and overwhelmed.

Setting a Goal to Get Along

I never thought my past would still be affecting me in my daily life today, but I get very depressed when I'm reminded of what I went through. My friends ask what's wrong, but I fear telling them that my past is haunting me. What if they don't understand? I hope I'll start to open up, though, because the anger that rises up in me is making it hard to be close to the people who care about me.

Recently I realized that over the 12 years I've been living with my adoptive mother, Lorine, I have been angry at her much of the time. Sometimes I've felt like a parent abusing my kid because I'm so furious. After I turn my anger on those who don't deserve to walk the plank of my wrath, I feel guilty and foolish, especially when others make bad remarks about my outbursts.

It seems as if my anger has become a habit that's grown too powerful for me to cope with. Being angry at the world is not helping me. So in the fall I set a goal of learning to settle conflicts without catching a short fuse, and to stop letting my anger control me and disrupt my relationships. I would like to have a better relationship with my mother, and to communicate better with my friends.

Getting Into It With My Mother

My mother and I usually argue about my friends. She preaches at me because she thinks my friends are a bad influence. Sometimes I'm curious—why doesn't she trust me to choose good friends? Is she trying to help me think about what's best for me, or does she think that I don't deserve to have friends?

But when we're talking, I don't act curious. I just feel upset and I rarely listen to what she says. At times like that, I can't tell if my mother is trying to protect me or hurt me. Once I start to defend myself, we fight.

'You're a Punk'

Even with my friends, I notice myself starting arguments, usually because I feel insecure about our friendship.

One time my friend Damion and I were hanging out, but I felt he was ignoring me so I got mad at him and said I was leaving. Damion wanted an explanation. He said, "What's your problem?"

I said in return, "I don't know." From there, we argued and I called him a punk.

Then Damion spoke his mind about me and my anger. He said, "We used to laugh and joke around, but you've changed. You get angry and say I'm not a good friend to you. Well, I'm not going to be speaking to you until you learn to get your priorities straight, and get rid of that anger of yours."

Ashamed of My Anger

I started to feel bad that I was so angry with Damion without a good reason. I started crying because I'd lost a valuable friend. If I'd told him calmly why I felt sad, our friendship would've been fine. But I just had to open my mouth and call him a name.

After that, we didn't speak for two days. On the third day, I decided to let him know that I was wrong for calling him a punk. I was hoping he'd forgive me and just start over, but he hesitated. He wasn't sure he was ready to forgive me, or that he could trust me again.

Eventually we talked our problems over and put the past behind us. But I still felt bad that Damion was paying a price for my past.

Help From a Book

To find out how to calm down my anger, I bought a book called The Anger Habit. It explains that anger is not a good way to handle problems or communicate, and shows other ways to solve disputes.

Reading the book made me think practically. I decided that no matter what's troubling me, I shouldn't act out in rage. I should remember that there are other ways for me to respond, and remind myself that getting angry only makes communication more difficult and relationships worse. So even if I'm feeling angry inside, I shouldn't express it by erupting at those who are dearest to me.

'I Don't Want to Argue With You'

I decided that when situations get upsetting, the best thing I can do is walk away and try to calm down before returning to the conversation.

When my mother got upset, I would say, "I'm not going to argue with you." Then I'd walk away. My mother understood why I did that. She began to see that our arguments didn't change my behavior. If anything, they made me more set in my ways.

I also began to put my anger into my poems instead of lashing out. For a while, I spent most of my time writing down my thoughts. In my poems, I acknowledged that my anger was a major problem for me and everyone around me. I wrote about suffering while growing up, and about trying to heal myself through poetry and by changing my behavior.

One night when I was in bed, I told myself, "Getting so angry isn't worth it anymore." I imagined having a happy look on my face day to day, and looking back at my teenage years wondering, "That was me acting like that? I'm glad that my stormy days are over."

Imagining my future made me feel free. Reading my book and practicing not getting angry made me feel like I was in Anger School taking anger-reduction classes to graduate. If I didn't meet the requirements of reducing my anger, I wouldn't be able to reach happiness. If I did do my homework, I'd get to see the future I wanted for myself.

Getting an Apology

When I tried to handle conflicts with Damion more calmly, our relationship got stronger.

Damion and I had some troubles after he moved. Suddenly he didn't call me as much as he said he would. I called him a few times and left messages. I started to get very upset and wondered if he was lying to me about being my friend.

The next time I called him, I left a message explaining that I was hurt: "Hey, this is Eric. What happened to you, Damion? Why are you not calling me like you said you would? If you say you're going to call me, then call me."

What I said was a little angry, but mostly sad.

Seconds later, Damion called me and apologized.

Soon he was calling me more often.

Gaining Control

It hasn't been easy to make such a big change. Sometimes I still get into arguments with my mother, even though I promised myself that I would no longer get angry.

The arguments are usually about the freedom that I want. I don't mean for them to become arguments. At the beginning of the conversation, I just want to know her reasons for not giving me the freedom I feel I deserve. But when my mother gives her reasons, it feels like too much criticism. Then I defend myself by telling my mother that I'm old enough to make my own decisions.

I want to listen to my mother, but that's a hard topic for us. It hurts my feelings when she acts like I'm not trustworthy, even though I'm trying to be. Still, our arguments aren't as intense as in the past.

Getting Closer to Mom and Dad

Since my behavior shifted gears, my home life has begun to feel more peaceful and less out of control. My parents have both noticed how hard I've been trying, and now we talk a lot more than we used to.

Before, I wouldn't talk to them. I would say just a few words and walk away. Now I talk and help them out more. Just the other day my mother and I were talking about Jerry Springer and how the guests fight and look stupid on TV. We were laughing and joking around, and for a moment, it didn't feel as if we were mother and son. It felt like we were friends.

My adoptive dad and I usually didn't talk much either. I cut conversations short because I didn't think he'd care what I said.

But lately I've been having long conversations with him, whether it's about my brother's nasty attitude or just about what I saw outside. Now that we're talking more, I feel different. I feel like I'm building the closeness with my family that I used to try to get by fighting.

Of course, my relationships with my parents and friends aren't perfect. But I feel proud of myself for trying to drop the load of anger I've been carrying with me. Even though it's going to take some time before I'm truly calm, I know I'm going in the right direction.

About Youth Communication

Youth Communication, founded in 1980, is nonprofit educational publishing company located in New York City. Our mission is to help marginalized youth develop their full potential through reading and writing, so that they can succeed in school and at work and contribute to their communities.

Youth Communication publishes true stories by teens that are developed in a rigorous writing program. We offer more than 50 books that adults can use to engage reluctant teen readers on an array of topics including peer pressure, school, sex, and relationships. Our stories also appear in our two award-winning magazines, *YCteen* and *Represent*, and on our website (www.youthcomm.org), and are frequently reprinted in popular and professional magazines and textbooks. We offer hundreds of lessons, complete leader's guides (like this one), and professional development to guide educators in using the stories to help teens improve their academic, social, and emotional skills.

Our stories, written by a diverse group of writers, are uniquely compelling to peers who do not see their experiences reflected in mainstream reading materials. They motivate teens to read and write, encourage good values, and show teens how to make positive changes in their lives.

You can access many of our stories and sample lessons for free at www.youthcomm.org. For more information on our products and services, contact Loretta Chan at 212-279-0708 x115, or lchan@youthcomm.org.

Youth Communication®
224 W. 29th St, 2nd Fl.
New York, NY 10001
212-279-0708
www.youthcomm.org

For Teens & Teachers
HELPFUL BOOKS FROM

YOUTH COMMUNICATION
Read. Write. Succeed.

The Struggle to Be Strong:
True Stories About Overcoming Tough Times
Book, 179pp.,
ISBN #9781575420790,
$13.95*

Young people will be inspired to identify and build on their own strengths with these 30 personal stories about resiliency.

Real Men:
Urban Teens Write About How to Be a Man
Book, 226 pp.,
ISBN #9781935552437,
$16.95*

An anthology of 32 true stories by male teens on how they have overcome challenges to success, such as negative self-image, unstable family life, difficult emotions, and dropping out of school.

Foreword by Geoffrey Canada

TEACHERS! LEADER'S GUIDES are available for all three books. Go to www.youthcomm.org for more info.

Real Jobs, Real Stories:
Stories by Teens About Succeeding at Work
Book, 179 pp.,
ISBN # 9781933939964,
$16.95*

In this collection of 33 true stories, teens describe how they got jobs, how they kept them, and what they learned. They also write about managing the money they earned, and how they are planning for the future.

*Discounts for Group Orders
Ordering 20 or more copies of a title?
Contact us at Lchan@youthcomm.org
or 212-279-0708 x115 for more information.

Order Form

Ship To: (No P.O. Boxes)
Name_____
Title_____
Organization_____
Address_____
City_____ State_____ Zip_____
Phone/e-mail_____

Payment Information
☐ Check Enclosed
☐ Credit Card (circle one): Visa/Master Card   Amex   Discover
Card #_____ Exp date_____

_____
Cardholder name exactly as it appears on card (please print)

_____
Cardholder Signature

Title	Price	Quantity	Total
The Struggle...	$13.95	____	____
Real Men	$16.95	____	____
Real Jobs, Real Stories	$16.95	____	____

Shipping & Handling → Shipping _____
(10% of Subtotal)   Total _____

Return order form to: Youth Communication, 224 W. 29th St., 2nd fl., New York, NY 10001, Tel: 212-279-0708 x. 115, FAX 212-279-8856

Order online today at: **www.youthcomm.org**

MANAGING TRANSITIONS FOR TEENS

Teen Journal: Managing Transitions for Teens
Book, 178 pp., ISBN #9781935552727, $12.95*

This Teen Journal (and the whole Transitions program) can help you learn how to manage transitions in your life, so you can take more control over what's happening. You'll learn about the stages people go through when they're facing a change, and try out lots of strategies to make the process easier. When you finish the workshop, this journal will be a record of everything you've accomplished, and a blueprint you can use to help you handle transitions in the future.

FOR TEENS

A Leader's Guide to Managing Transitions for Teens
Book, 122 pp.,
ISBN #9781935552710, $16.95*

Over 16 sessions, you'll engage teens in learning about the different stages of transition and the tools they can use to cope. And you'll help them apply those tools to a real transition they are trying to make in their lives. The strategies they learn in this workshop will help them in all of the future changes they face, from leaving the system to moving to new jobs, homes, or relationships.

FOR TEACHERS & STAFF

*Discounts for Group Orders
Ordering 20 or more copies of a title?
Contact us at Lchan@youthcomm.org
or 212-279-0708 x115 for more information.

Order Form

Ship To: (No P.O. Boxes)
Name_____
Title_____
Organization_____
Address_____
City_____ State_____ Zip_____
Phone/e-mail_____

Payment Information
☐ Check Enclosed
☐ Credit Card (circle one): Visa/Master Card   Amex   Discover
Card#_____ Exp date_____
_____
Cardholder name exactly as it appears on card (please print)
_____
Cardholder Signature

Title	Price	Quantity	Total
Transitions: Teen Journal	$12.95	_____	_____
Transitions: Leader's Guide	$16.95	_____	_____

Shipping & Handling → Shipping _____
(10% of Subtotal)
Total _____

Return order form to: Youth Communication,
224 W. 29th St., 2nd fl., New York, NY 10001,
Tel: 212-279-0708 x. 115, FAX 212-279-8856

Read. Write. Succeed.

Order online today at: www.youthcomm.org

www.ingramcontent.com/pod-product-compliance
Lightning Source LLC
Chambersburg PA
CBHW081357040426
42451CB00018B/3486